THE
WELSHPOOL & LLANFAIR
LIGHT RAILWAY

by

RALPH CARTWRIGHT

&

R. T. RUSSELL

DAVID & CHARLES
NEWTON ABBOT LONDON

British Library Cataloguing in Publication Data

Cartwright, R. I.
   The Welshpool & Llanfair Light Railway. –
   3rd ed.
   1. Powys. Montgomery (District). Narrow
   gauge railway services, to 1989
   I. Title   II. Russell, R.T.
   385'.52'0942951

   ISBN 0-7153-9226-3

First published 1972
Second edition 1981
Revised and updated edition 1989

© Ralph Cartwright and R. T. Russell 1972,
1981, 1989

Printed in Great Britain
by Redwood Burn Limited
Trowbridge, Wiltshire
for David & Charles Publishers plc
Brunel House Newton Abbot Devon

Contents

List of Illustrations

PLATES

v

IN TEXT

Authors' Notes

In this account, the authors aim to provide an authenticated, detailed study of a unique railway—one of the earliest progeny of the Light Railways Act of 1896 and the first example of such a line being taken over by preservationists. An attempt has been made to base this narrative throughout on original research and little recourse has been made to existing published works on the line's history. What was probably the first serious attempt to piece together the story was that of the late Lewis Cozens in his booklet *The Welshpool & Llanfair Light Railway* (1951) and acknowledgement is made of its use for suggesting lines of investigation. For background material, readers are directed to *The Cambrian Railways* by R. W. Kidner (1965 edition) and *The Cambrian Railways Vols I & II* by Rex Christianson & R. W. Miller (1967).

We are most grateful for help received in various ways from the following, some of whom are fortunate enough to have known the line in its commercial years either as employee or passenger: C. H. Betts of Ilford, G. R. Croughton of Sevenoaks, J. Cummings of Edgware, H. Evans of Oswestry, W. Gough of Welshpool, C. C. Green of Birmingham, Stanley H. Keyse also of Birmingham, G. S. Lodwick of Maesbury, Jack Pritchard of Welshpool, Mrs E. A. Scott of Eastbourne, J. P. Williams of Welshpool and E. Wilkinson of Newport (Mon.). Recent surveys of the line by the Department of Civil Engineering, University of Birmingham, were made available by the courtesy of R. G. Bird.

Thanks are due for the facilities offered so helpfully by the National Library of Wales, Aberystwyth, the British Transport Historical Records, Paddington and the Public Record Offices in London and Berkhamstead. Mention must be made of the invaluable assistance of the former Oswestry Public Library and Newtown Free Library, particularly in making available files and microfilm of local newspapers. In connection with the account of the locomotives and rolling stock, Mr R. T. Russell received

viii

much appreciated assistance from Messrs W. G. Bagnall Ltd (Stafford), A. Barclay, Sons and Co Ltd (Kilmarnock), the Hunslet Engine Co Ltd (Leeds) and D. Wickham and Co Ltd (Ware), while British Railways (Western Region) kindly provided drawings and locomotive workshop manuals.

We would like to record our gratitude for the interest of Mr Michael M. Polglaze, general manager of the railway in earlier years, and for his efforts in unearthing a number of long forgotten documents.

Acknowledgement is made of the kind co-operation of local officers of British Railways. Other people including many members of the preservation company have rendered assistance, and though the limitations of space and the blurring of memory precludes the listing of everyone, our appreciation is no less sincere.

Finally, wife Maureen Cartwright deserves considerable thanks for her understanding and encouragement while the work was in progress, in addition to making the MSS more acceptable by typing much of the final draft.

THE ILLUSTRATIONS

We are greatly indebted to Michael Christensen for his painstaking work on the many line drawings in the text. Other help has been given by I. McBriar and J. D. How. D. Fullwood kindly photographed the medals. The authors would like to thank the following for permission to use photographs from their cameras or their collections:

J. E. Cartwright, 13; R. A. Castle, 8; J. Clemmens, 18; R. Cragg, 24; John A. N. Emslie (R. Y. Pickering collection), 30, 33; C. Gammell, 14; C. C. Green, 1, 29; R. Johnson, 9; R. Murman, 31; Ivo Peters, 16; B. Roberts, 12; J. Tennant, 4; E. Thomas, 6; F. Wakelam, 7; G. A. Yeomans, 19; Welshpool Corporation (Powysland Museum Collection), 3; W & LLR Preservation Co Ltd, 2, 5, 10, 20, 25, 32. The remainder of the photographs are by the authors. The numbers refer to the list on page v.

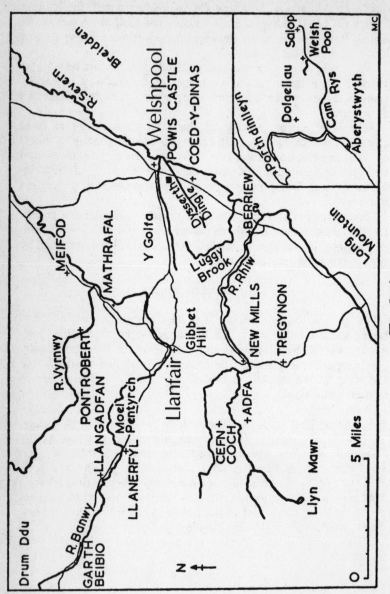

The Setting

TREN LLANFAIR

(The Llanfair Train)

Once, Welshpool town welcomed 'the Llanfair train' into its very heart. The Lilliputian wagons and tram-style coaches mingled with the borough's thoroughfares, bridged its brook and thrust through the tangle of backyards. Nowadays, the Welshpool and Llanfair Light Railway stands abruptly truncated on the west of the conglomeration of huddled houses. But beyond, lie the high moorlands of eastern Wales and happily, these slopes still resound to the canorous shriek of the two, chubby, stalwart o–6–o tank locomotives which provided, one at a time, all the motive power that was required during the line's working life.

Their sinuous, climbing, narrow gauge way threads the border heights to Llanfair Caereinion, once a railhead for an unquarried, unmined, upland world of scattered sheeptenders. Now, Llanfair is something of a tourist spot and the Mecca for thousands who have found the W & L and come to love it. The squat, little train wears a plume of steam and smoke as it sets off to court the rippling, smiling Afon Banwy. It rolls and turns and crosses from one side to the other as unhurriedly as it did for the first time over three quarters of a century ago. But few of its present-day passengers muse much over the way the original W & L translated a late eighteenth century concept into Welsh steel, creosoted lengths of pine and corrugated iron. In a region which could not sustain a full size branch railway and the usual main line trappings, money from Westminster, from the councils of Mid-Wales and from the local populace induced an appropriately basic 2ft 6in gauge line. Crossing all highways on the level, ungated in the usual way, unsignalled, it charged full tilt at the upland in its path. Ascents on the line include the steepest ever worked by the old Cambrian Railways.

The slow and friendly, make-do-and-mend, wait-for-anyone Light Railway atmosphere was retained and embraced when revival came in recent years. However, new and novel features have emerged. When the hurried, unrelenting puffing up Dolarddyn bank is cut off, into grassy Castle station may coast a formidable continental o–8–oT, embellished with a plethora of outside fittings. Behind, rumbles a rake of match-board-sided end-balconied vintage Austrian coaches. A new generation crams the balconies; the basket-laden market-bound lilting Welsh wives have given way to camera-swinging, brochure-hugging, wide-eyed visitors with a variety of accents. Today, as the new W & L operates its rather remarkable service of busy trains in each summer season, one remembers that it is dependent on—and is a tribute to—the voluntary efforts of many well-wishers who have joined the preservation company, all drawn together in a pioneering spirit. Though there have been crises and disappointments and things have often seemed to be moving slowly, determination and perseverence have prevailed in the end. Throughout the railway's history this has been so, as we shall see.

CHAPTER ONE

A Century of Railway Schemes

BACKGROUND

Where the wayward River Severn prepares to exchange its mountainous Montgomeryshire homeland for the vast plains of Shropshire, it enters a flat, fertile and well-defined corridor. Here the thirteenth-century borough of Welshpool nestles strategically, only three miles inside the Welsh border. Here, traffic is channelled between the Long Mountain and the Cambrian Massif as Welshpool marks the meeting of east and west, of English plain and Welsh mountain, of arable regime and pastoral economy. Westwards, stretch ridge after ridge of the Berwyn Mountains, rounded off rather below 2000 feet. There, on Drum Ddu, several tinkling streams rise to descend and unite as the stone-strewn Afon Banwy which plunges inland towards Welshpool. Beside the banks of this capricious river is hidden the small township of Llanfair Caereinion, flanked by steep-sided hills to north and south.

The easy outlet eastwards is soon frustrated when the peevish River Banwy bends sharply northwards, turning a cold shoulder to the Severn a few miles away and going on to dally with the Afon Vyrnwy in the picturesque Vale of Meifod. To reach Welshpool, there is thus the valley side to climb before the watershed is gained in the Pass of Golfa at 620ft above sea-level, between the crests of Pen-y-foel and Y Golfa. A steep descent then follows beside the stream known first as the Sylfaen Brook, then as the Nant-y-caws Brook and in Welshpool as the Lledan Brook. A less direct route between Welshpool and Llanfair uses the 700ft gap to the south immediately behind the village of Castle Caereinion but this also involves a considerable climb.

Lying on the old road from Shrewsbury to Aberystwyth, Llanfair Caereinion grew up as a market centre for the area of central moorlands. It experienced industrial prosperity for a brief span a century ago, at the same time as the inns were busy with drovers. Then, they came for Llanfair's fairs or were herding pigs or Welsh Black cattle towards the English Midlands. But even when Llanfair's trading function was increasing in importance, communications remained tedious. Packhorses were much used and teams of donkeys hauled coal from Welshpool. The coach services to and from the Welsh coast braved the rutted, muddy roads twice weekly in winter and thrice in summer. At last, in 1851, a carrier began the first daily service from Llanfair to Welshpool.

For over 700 years, Welshpool's chief attraction for border people has been its market, held regularly on Mondays, bank holidays notwithstanding. Its industries have included malting, tanning and flannel weaving while the now disused Standard Quarry and, out of town, the long-working Buttington brickworks and Briedden quarries stand as evidence of other industrial activity.

TRAMROADS

Communications for Welshpool and its hinterland began to improve when the Ellesmere and Montgomeryshire Canals were built. By 1797, the system extended south to Welshpool and some five miles beyond, facilitating the import of Denbighshire coal and Llanymynech lime. Under the Ellesmere and Montgomeryshire Canal Acts of 1793-4, powers were granted for the building of rail feeders up to three miles in length to connect with the new waterway. Promoted by Welshpool's Earl of Powis (probably Edward, 2nd Lord Clive), five such tramways were laid in the area between Welshpool and Llynclys (south of Oswestry).

It is of interest that the 2ft 6in gauge came to the area as early as the beginning of the nineteenth century. It was chosen for the most northerly of the five tramways, the Porthywaen Iron Railway. For a hundred years, four or five horse-drawn trains conveyed limestone daily from the Porthywaen Quarries to a run-round loop on the fairly spacious

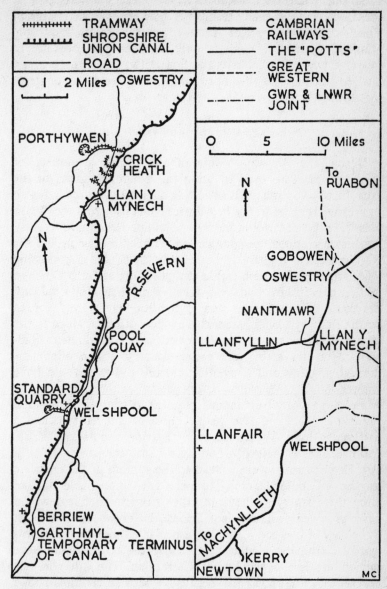

+++++++++ TRAMWAY
.... SHROPSHIRE
          UNION CANAL
———————— ROAD

O I 2 Miles

———— CAMBRIAN
      RAILWAYS
———— THE "POTTS"
- - - - GREAT
         WESTERN
-·-·-·- GWR & LNWR
         JOINT

O   5   10 Miles

OSWESTRY

PORTHYWAEN

CRICK
HEATH

LLAN Y
MYNECH

N

R. SEVERN

POOL
QUAY

STANDARD
QUARRY

WELSHPOOL

BERRIEW

GARTHMYL -
TEMPORARY TERMINUS
OF CANAL

N

To
RUABON

GOBOWEN
OSWESTRY

NANTMAWR

LLANFYLLIN

LLAN Y
MYNECH

LLANFAIR

WELSHPOOL

To MACHYNLLETH

KERRY

NEWTOWN

MC

(*left*) Before the railway era, c.1797 (*right*) Railway development
by 1866

canal-side wharf at Crickheath village. The southern-most of the Earl's fan of canal tramways was the Welsh Pool Rail Road, constructed about 1817 to carry granite from the Standard Quarry. Though it only survived just over thirty years, it was remarkable as the first railway anywhere to use chaired track and significant in that it indicated a way of cleaving through the town beside the Lledan Brook.

DREAMS AND REALITIES

During the Railway Mania of the 1840s, a number of schemes were proposed to bring rail communications to the area. In 1845, Isambard Kingdom Brunel drew up plans for an impressive scheme to lay broad gauge metals across the Welsh massif. Fulfilment would have put Llanfair Caereinion in early possession of good communication with both London and the west coast. Once already, however, a GWR plan for crossing Wales to carry the Irish traffic to a new port at Porth Dinlleyn in Caernarvonshire had been frustrated when Holyhead and the route of the Chester and Crewe Railway were favoured by the Railway Commissioners. This new attempt, allied to the GWR cause, was called the Worcester and Porthdinlleyn Railway. After traversing the easier country on an alignment through Ludlow and Craven Arms, the railway would have entered Montgomeryshire before being carried through the Aran range with tremendous feats of cutting, bridging and tunnelling including two major bores each over two and a half miles long. Westward from Berriew (south of Welshpool), Brunel envisaged a five mile climb steepening to 1 in 103. Deep cuttings were to lead to the summit at the entrance to the 1½ mile Llanfair tunnel. The appreciable incline into the Banwy valley in the tunnel confines would have provided fearsome conditions for crews on the open footplates of the early engines, especially those slogging eastward. A dramatic viaduct, 92ft above the river, would have carried the line over Llanfair Caereinion. The Bill was not proceeded with, apparently because it became certain in 1846 that Parliament was to prohibit new broad gauge construction. There is little doubt that cost would anyway have militated against completion.

Page 17 *CONSTRUCTION*
(above) Strachan No 3: *the contractor's standard gauge locomotive on the site of Welshpool goods yard;* (below) *building underpass for cattle, Golfa bank, 1901*

Page 18 *CAMBRIAN DAYS*

(above) *Opening day 1903: at the original terminus in Smithfield Road, Welshpool. Directors of the* W & L *on right;*
(below) *a train for Llanfair filling up at the early water tower close to Dolrhyd Mill*

A rival standard gauge scheme was also mooted. In August 1845, *The Railway Times* included details of the Great Welsh Junction Company which envisaged a grandiose system connecting Bangor and Porth Dynlleyn with South Wales, and having a trunk line from Dolgellau through or close to Llanfair Caereinion, to Welshpool and eastwards. Like many of the 620 schemes quoted as having been proposed that year, it was wound up. The scheme which was eventually successful in bringing the first railway to Montgomeryshire was the Oswestry, Welchpool and Newtown Railway, proposed in 1854. Tremendous ceremony marked the opening at Welshpool on 4 August 1860, although ten months passed before the line was completed right through to Newtown.

Within the next few years, a great deal of agitation arose for railway connections for many small towns and villages in the vicinity, possession of a railway being regarded by many people in the Welsh valleys as something of a panacea. The busy market centre of Llanfair Caereinion (population 2584) was no exception. Demand for improved communications with the lowlands was fanned by the introduction of daily services to Welshpool by horse-bus or wagonette, although the nine mile journey was slow and uncomfortable. The first wagonettes used offered patrons little protection from the elements. Indeed it is reputed that one poor soul froze to death en route on one occasion! The services were soon arranged to connect with the mid-morning and evening trains at Welshpool, but those who were obliged to transfer from rail to road must have been acutely aware of the shortcomings of the only available means of public transport to Llanfair.

The summer months of 1862 saw a definite scheme being hatched out for a railway from Welshpool, the motivation being provided chiefly by Abraham Howell (a solicitor, and the mayor of Welshpool), Capt Pryce (of Cyfronydd), Major Davis (of Brnglass) and Charles Humphreys (of Llanfair). The proposed route was from Welshpool station, across the canal near the Smithfield Market, by tunnel under the town and on to Llanfair via Golfa. At a public meeting in Llanfair, the inhabitants were told that a possible route southwards from Welshpool (via Dysserth) was impracticable and a route

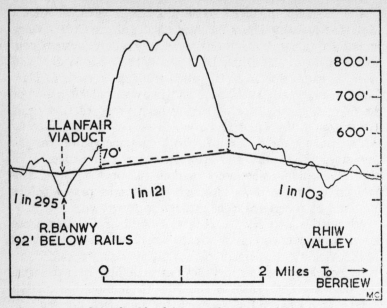

LLANFAIR
VIADUCT

70'

1 in 295

1 in 121

1 in 103

800' —

700' —

600' —

R.BANWY
92' BELOW RAILS

RHIW
VALLEY

0   1   2 Miles To ⟶
                              BERRIEW

MC

Brunel's Llanfair tunnel scheme, 1845

from Llanfair to Llanfyllin via Meifod was too indirect. The
Earl of Powis nevertheless objected to the proposed route
which would have interfered with a favourite road of his.
In September, however, a new route was announced, largely
'suggested by the Earl'. This was the Dysserth route, starting
from the Oswestry and Newtown Railway, three furlongs south
of Welshpool, and skirting the south-eastern flanks of the
Powis estate to reach Castle Caereinion and continue to Llanfair on the south bank of the River Banwy. Not only did this
remove the Earl's earlier opposition but it avoided the
expensive necessity of tunnelling to get past the centre of
Welshpool which occupied the gap between two hills.

Further public meetings were held in 1862 and it seems
that the idea was for a standard gauge branch to be made by a
main-line company, at a possible cost of £50,000. The branch
would have run at least to Llanfair, perhaps even to Machynlleth, with landowners as far as possible taking shares in
payment for their land. Heralding a dispute which was to
reach its height thirty-five years later, there was already a
lack of unanimity with regard to the route, some being in

favour of a railway from Llanfair leading to Newtown via Forden and others of using the Meifod valley to reach Llansantffraid. The committee consulted David Davies (1818–90) of Llandinam, currently being acclaimed for his feats of construction on the main-line railways of Wales, but the scheme did not recommend itself to him as a sound business proposition. Thus the matter ended, at least for the time being.

THE FIRST NARROW GAUGE SCHEME

In 1864 Abraham Howell (1810–93), who had taken a prominent part in the promotion of the railways which were to become the backbone of the Cambrian, decided to persuade David Davies to re-examine the scheme he had earlier condemned. One summer's day they set out together to walk over the route past Trefnant Hall, up the Luggy Brook and over the summit. Despite the splendour of the Dysserth woods and the magnificence of the views on the descent into the Banwy valley, the expedition only served to convince Davies that his prognostication had been correct. It was a month or two later that an event took place which inspired

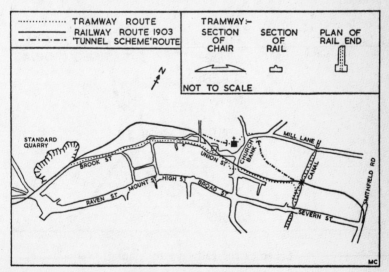

Routes through Welshpool

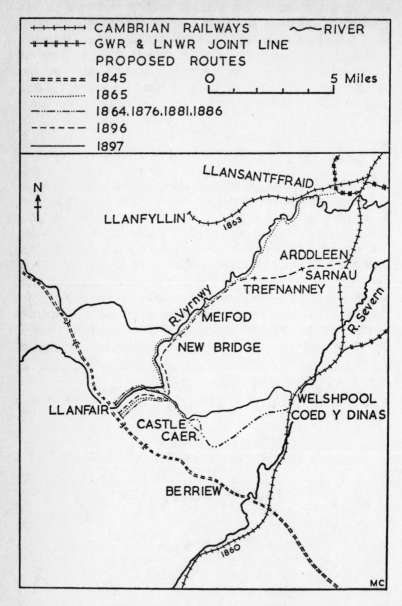

Schemes for railways to Llanfair

him with a solution. Over the mountains at Portmadoc, the
Festiniog Railway, of only 1ft 11½in gauge, was experiment-
ing with steam locomotives after nearly thirty years of slate
carrying by gravity and horse. About this time, it was
inspected by Capt Tyler for the Board of Trade. Not only did
he pronounce it fit to carry passengers—the first line of less
than standard gauge to be so favoured—but he also commended the narrow gauge locomotives as an economic
proposition and an example to cheap lines in undeveloped
areas. Here, then, was a solution to help the people of Llanfair
Caereinion.

The influential gentlemen who had so far been frustrated
in their efforts now saw their chance to promote a railway
which would be a viable proposition. By 30 November 1864,
they had deposited the plans, hoping soon to gain Parliamentary sanction and to be able to raise sufficient money to
construct the railway to a narrow gauge. The ten miles of
the 'Llanfair Railway', as they called it, were to start on the
south bank of the River Banwy close to Llanfair bridge.
Eastwards, the line would be close to the river as far as
Cyfronydd, rising then for over a mile at 1 in 45 to go under
the road at Dolarddyn before cutting round to the north of
Castle Caereinion village. It would then descend with long
stretches of steep gradients as severe as 1 in 40 via the Luggy
valley to the Oswestry and Newtown Railway about a mile
south of Welshpool. It was proposed to lay a third rail along
the main line and have running powers over mixed gauge
track into Welshpool station.

Having now prepared for Parliamentary action, it was
vital to ensure that financial support would be forthcoming.
At a meeting at Llanfair's Goat Inn soon afterwards, it was
explained that the scheme, including rolling stock, could be
carried through for £33,000. Optimistic though the promoters
were, their hopes were once more dashed for by the spring
of 1865 it became apparent that support would be insufficient.
There were those who scorned anything less than 4ft 8½in,
while the newly formed Cambrian Railways Company was
quick to disown any affiliation. So lapsed a scheme for what
might have been only the second passenger carrying narrow
gauge line in the country.

THE CHALLENGE FROM MEIFOD

Failure at this stage was also partly due to an alternative scheme which was being mooted, not for the first time nor by any means the last. The inhabitants of Meifod, five miles to the north east of Llanfair, were also anxious to have the benefits of rail communication. They felt that it was physically easier to construct a line of railway along their wide, flat valley floor and through the Banwy gap to Llanfair, while it would provide a more direct route to the limestone quarries, the North Wales coal mines and the stock markets at Oswestry and beyond. The Meifodians approached Mr Richard Samuel France, the owner of limestone quarries at Llanymynech, who was interested in railway construction, particularly where it gave him better distribution for his products. He was promoting the Shrewsbury and North Wales Railway, soon to become the Potteries, Shrewsbury and North Wales and later the Shropshire and Montgomeryshire Light Railway. During 1865, he was asked to add to his plans a lengthy, standard gauge branch from Careghofa near Llanymynech to Llanfair Caereinion. It was to pass on the south side of Llansantffraid, along the Vale of Meifod and up the side of the River Banwy, crossing to the south bank near Cyfronydd to reach a station close to the vicarage in Llanfair town. The ruling gradient would have been 1 in 100. By the time his Bill was being considered by a Parliamentary Committee in May 1866, Mr France was having to explain that the part relating to the Meifod extension was to be deleted due to the lack of funds to carry out its construction.

A LIGHT RAILWAY PROPOSITION

A number of years now elapsed before the next move. Towards the end of 1874, at a public meeting, the people of Caereinion debated the merits of the various proposed routes to Llanfair, agreed on the importance of unity and plumped for a scheme taking the same direction as the 1864 route— to Welshpool. In the following spring, under the Chairmanship of Capt R. D. Pryce (then deputy chairman of the Cambrian Railways), a Board was set up consisting of twenty-five landowners. It was planned to avoid any expenses for professional services, to get agreements with the landowners affected and gain promises of the necessary capital before going to Parliament. As the summer passed, over £17,000 was promised including a substantial amount from the Earl of Powis who was willing to allow the proposed line to cross his estate, and by the autumn the route was surveyed. Detailed plans were drawn up, this time for a standard gauge line to Welshpool, and further meetings were held at Llanfair to enlist support.

The new plan proposed to site the western terminus roughly where the present station is, with the main Welshpool road diverted to the river side of the station before climbing over the railway. The line itself would leave the station and, after diving under the present-day A 458 road, would then cross the river on a 90ft three-span bridge and continue along the southern bank. After leaving the Banwy valley, it was to climb into Castle Caereinion village, passing along the southern edge of the churchyard and descending to the Luggy Brook before skirting the southern fringes of the Dysserth and Powis estates and joining the Cambrian's Oswestry and Newton railway at Coed-y-dinas, a mile south of Welshpool. The scheme was to be accomplished for £40,000 which would be sufficient to build a light railway for working at a maximum speed of 20mph—a prophetic touch in view of the Light Railway Order quarter of a century later. LNWR and Cambrian Railways' trains were envisaged running over it, and being subjected to this limit. Had the Cambrian opposed the plans, the promoters were prepared to seek powers to construct their own line alongside the Cambrian Railways main line into Welshpool to a station of their own but, apart from a spur for a terminal, these powers were not found to be necessary.

AUTHORISED . . . AND ABANDONED

On 10 August 1877, an Act authorised the construction of a railway from near Welshpool to Llanfair. The line was to

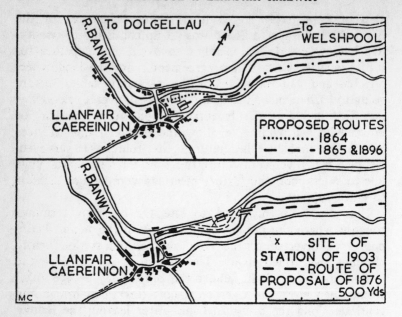

Proposed termini. (*above*) Llanfair. (*below*) Welshpool

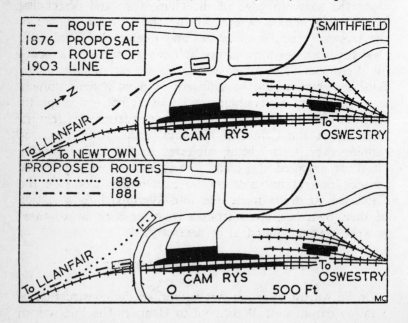

be 9 miles 5 furlongs long, with an interchange siding for the use of the Dysserth estate and could be worked by the Cambrian Railways Company. A clause had been inserted authorising the construction of a new carriage road from Pont Sychcoed (Cyfronydd bridge) to Mathrafal Castle on the Meifod road to give convenient access from the vale to the north. Yet even with such a sop to the Meifodians, insufficient financial support was forthcoming. Some of the residents of Llanfair had been rather half-hearted in their backing, and as time went by—five years were allowed by the Act for construction—it seemed that the powers at last granted would lapse. It would anyway have been a difficult and expensive line to work with gradients as steep as 1 in 44 and 1 in 51 approaching Castle Caereinion from the Welshpool side and two and half miles of 1 in 64 to reach the village from the west.

But now events took place which were almost a repetition of those of 1864. In 1881, with time running out, the promoters saw an example on the west coast of what they must do. Four years previously the North Wales Narrow Gauge Railway, the Welsh Highland of later years, had opened a line of similar length. The figures available for their train mileage and working expenses convinced the Montgomeryshire promoters that they would be able to pay a 4½ per cent dividend on capital of £34,000 which was the estimated cost, including rolling stock, of a narrow gauge line to Llanfair. They argued that a narrow gauge line could be built more cheaply with easier gradients and they hoped receipts would approach the £3,676 of the Llanfyllin branch in 1880 (a depression year) against working expenses in line with the £2,131 of the North Wales Narrow Gauge Railway for that year. They were now able to gain the support of most landowners and promises to take up shares were invited on the understanding that the scheme would be abandoned if less than £22,500 was secured, the Earl of Powis lending his support by taking up £4,000 in shares. Preparations were made to get authority for the change of gauge, to extend the time allowed under the Act for construction and to run the narrow gauge metals into Welshpool to a terminus just south of the main line station. But subscriptions still flagged and in the 1882 Parliamentary session, authority was granted for total abandonment of the 1877 scheme.

ANOTHER NARROW GAUGE VENTURE

Some of the leading figures in the struggle for a railway into Caereinion lost heart, including Capt R. D. Pryce of Cyfronydd whose death was near. But moves now started outside the area, ostensibly to help the people of this part of Mid-Wales to secure what they needed but could not themselves afford. A firm of civil engineers, Simpson, Davies and Hurst of London, were behind this proposition, the latter appearing at a public meeting in the Cross Foxes Hotel at Llanfair Caereinion on 8 October 1886 and promising to raise the balance of the cost if local support could be obtained to the tune of £15,000. Comparisons were again made to persuade the gathered residents of the viability of narrow gauge construction, and the whole scheme was to cost £40,000. It was to be just over 10 miles in length, again with its own station in Welshpool just across the road on the west of the Cambrian's. Leaving the side of the main line at Coed-y-dinas, it was to strike out for the Luggy Brook and pass south of Castle Caereinion, crossing the Dolarddyn road on a 25ft span bridge before following the line of the later Light Railway construction. Gradients were to be as steep as ever, including a mile at 1 in 40.

The narrow gauge was becoming more acceptable and, in an editorial column, the *Oswestry Advertizer and Border Counties Herald* enthusiastically advocated support for the latest Llanfair Railway scheme. Parliamentary processes now took their course and on 23 August 1887, sanction was given for the construction. Care was to be exercised as to the manner in which the railway crossed the Montgomeryshire Canal near Coed-y-dinas, with regard to the Earl of Powis' private drive en route and in the Dysserth Estate with its valuable timber. Although five years were again allowed for completion of the line, contributions once more looked like falling short of the necessary total and the promoters lost interest in favour of potentially more profitable schemes which they departed to survey.

The unsuccessful efforts to provide a railway for the people of Llanfair Caereinion over the last thirty years had proved, if nothing else, that the Powysians must accept a line of quite steep gradients and low overall speeds. Even then, the only project likely to be effective must be economically built on the shortest possible route—a narrow gauge connection to the east—and financial help from outside was essential. On the horizon, there was now appearing the means to provide just that extra source of finance which events had shown to be required. In the nineties, a new Railway Act was anticipated in the valleys of eastern Wales, as in other places, with hopes of rail communications for all and sundry. In the hills to the south, Tregynon and neighbouring villages, small as they were, were talking of a Bechan Valley Light Railway emanating from Newtown and running within three miles of Llanfair Caereinion. Nothing came of it, for on the northern flanks of Gibbet Hill the time was at long last almost ripe for a line of metals to penetrate the heart of this captivating hill region.

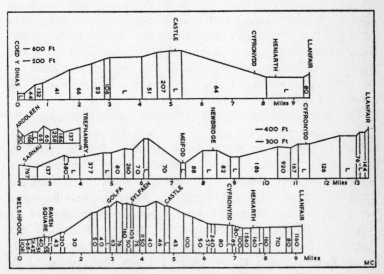

Light railways: proposed gradient profiles
(*above*) W & LLR, authorised 1877 (*centre*) Llanfair & Meifod LR, proposed 1896 (*below*) W & LLR authorised 1899

CHAPTER TWO

The Light Railway is Planned

NEW LEGISLATION

The idea of legislation to foster the construction of simple lines of railway to serve country areas was one in which there was mounting interest in the Welsh Marchlands during the last decade of the nineteenth century. Private enterprise had failed to provide improved communications for these farming communities with slender financial resources. In November 1895, some of the populace of Llanfair Caereinion met to frame a resolution for their Member of Parliament (A. C. Humphreys-Owen) to take to London. They asked for action by the Government, and shortly afterwards they arranged for a similar demand to be sent to HM Treasury and various Members of Parliament. They hoped that it would become lawful for public funds, both central and local, to be directed towards railway construction—particularly, of course, of a line to Llanfair.

The agitation was to bear fruit. On 14 August 1896, the Light Railways Act became law. It was an early attempt to 'develop' hitherto economically backward areas by publicly subsidising communications. Finance could be provided, within prescribed limits, from Treasury funds (up to half the total cost) and by local authority subscriptions. Expenses were cut by abolishing the need to obtain authorisation by Act of Parliament, a Parliamentary Order confirmed by the Board of Trade now being sufficient. Furthermore, railways so authorised were to be exempt from the provisions of various Railway Acts in the interests of economy. In view of such relaxations a relatively low overall speed limit was to be imposed, and junctions had to avoid interference with the rails of existing lines as far as possible. The financial assistance was conditional upon an existing railway company constructing and operating the Light Railway, while land for the lines had to be given free as far as possible and 'all reasonable assistance' by landowners was expected by the Act. Even before it reached the statute book, Powysians were optimistically calculating the benefits the Light Railways Act would bestow. Quick off the mark, meetings at Llanfair under the auspices of the Parish Council had appointed a committee which was planning a Light Railway before the end of 1895.

The committee's attention was initially drawn to a number of routes—to Welshpool station either by Golfa and through the town centre, or via Dysserth Dingle or via Berriew; to Pool Quay via Golfa and Guilsfield; and via Meifod to Four Crosses or Llanymynech. They visualised standard gauge trains working up the Banwy valley and their findings influenced the 300 parishoners who attended a meeting in May 1896 into deciding—still ahead of the passing of the new Act—upon the Meifod route. That the initiative should come from the people of Llanfair, and that they should apparently be in favour of a line to the north, irked townsfolk in Welshpool. Welshpool Town Council now realised that they, too, must act and appointed a committee to investigate and make recommendations.

THE RIVAL PLANS

Plans for the Llanfair and Meifod Light Railway were meanwhile taking shape. For an estimated £41,000, it was hoped to build a line, $13\frac{1}{2}$ miles in length, from a station in the vicarage field at Llanfair Caereinion, along the south bank of the river Banwy, past Pont-sychcoed (near Cyfronydd), through Meifod and up a mile-long stretch of 1 in 70 through Sarney to join the Oswestry and Welshpool main line at Arddleen. The chief personality behind the scheme was Dr C. E. Humphreys of Llanfair, who canvassed the surrounding area for support. In December 1896 the *Border Counties Advertizer*, reported the lodging of the application for a Light Railway Order, stating 'it was the first application from any part of Britain'.

In Welshpool, while news from their committee was awaited with impatience, various suggestions were voiced. Some were prompted by memories of earlier schemes such as that for a new road to approach Cyfronydd station from the north (to placate Meifodians) and that for a tunnel under part of Welshpool. By October the investigation committee was ready to report to the Town Council which was quick to put the matter to approving townspeople at a public meeting. With thoughts of the light railway system in Belgium in mind, a route was recommended by the roadside (except for the Smithfield Market—Church Street portion in Welshpool and the ascent of Golfa bank). Already, a gauge of 2ft 6in was mooted. It was commended for its economy, for its facility for sharp curves, for its suitability for extension westwards into the hills and for its capacity for comparatively powerful locomotives with suitable rail. First estimates of the cost of the scheme including rolling stock put it at £25,000. Messrs Moorsam and Ward, a Welshpool firm of engineers, prepared a survey of the route, now including a slight diversion across the fields to pass near the small farming community of Castle Caereinion (pop. 350).

On 28 January 1897 a meeting held in Welshpool Town Hall elected a promotion committee, consisting of no less than ninety local worthies including the whole of Welshpool Corporation and Castle Caereinion Parish Council. The chairman was William Forrester-Addie (1851–1921) who, for the second year running, was mayor of the town. The committee soon decided to adopt the projected 2ft 6in gauge and further resolved that the line should go through the Pass of Golfa, although it was not satisfied with the idea of following the 'turnpike road' as opposition was anticipated from the county council. It was agreed to divert the railway off the roadside all the way west of Raven Square—and also out of Brook Street in Welshpool. It was now to cut through the fields to the south of the road and cross the River Banwy, not at Cyfronydd, but as it neared Llanfair. A projected new street in Welshpool to provide a route for the line between Church Street and Brook Street would have involved the demolition of a dozen shops and houses, and was eventually scaled down to a narrow alley of which the longitudinal bridge over the

Lledan Brook was a continuation, the alley requiring the destruction of only three houses. To minimise delays to through rail traffic at Welshpool, the committee envisaged using transporter wagons. E. R. Calthrop was quoted as saying that transshipment by this means would only take three minutes.

The scheme was explained at Llanfair when a deputation led by Forrester-Addie met the Llanfair Parish Council in April, 1897. The division of support between rival schemes was obviously undesirable, but the parish councillors remained intransigent, the village doctor being particularly hypercritical of the Welshpool scheme. Rebuffed, the delegation returned to Welshpool. At 10.30 on the morning of 7 May 1897, they deposited their £50 with the Clerk to Montgomeryshire County Council together with their plans and application for an Order for a Light Railway of 9 miles 1 furlong and 1½ chains in length.

THE INQUIRY

The morning of Tuesday 3 August was fine and warm as a Great Western express with a through coach to Aberystwyth pulled out of Paddington station. Aboard were three

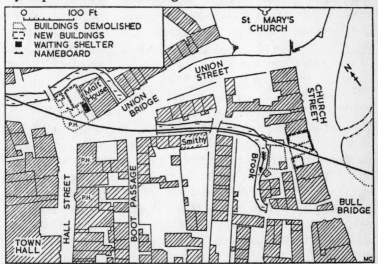

Squeezing through the town. Few buildings were demolished—
and some rebuilding was possible.

men on whose report depended the future of new railways in the Border country—the Earl of Jersey, Colonel Boughey RE and Mr G. A. R. Fitzgerald, all Light Railway Commissioners. Leaving the train at Welshpool, they reached Llanfair Caereinion to start, at 3.30pm, the official inquiry required by Section VII of the 1896 Light Railways Act. This was only the second inquiry held concerning a narrow gauge line. In the Board School, a large crowd from the surrounding area had gathered to hear the arguments to be put forward for and against the two rival schemes.

Having made their application first, the promoters of the proposed Llanfair and Meifod Light Railway appeared first. Backed by the Mayor of Oswestry, they detailed the support they had from the parish and district councils along the route. Mr Denniss spoke for the Cambrian Railways Company which was prepared to build and work the line. He expected to carry 26,000 passengers annually, 2,300 tons of coal and 3,600 tons of other goods. But now things began to go badly for the promoters. Horace Bell, late consulting engineer to the Indian Government, who had been retained by the Welshpool committee, was sceptical about the profitability of the traffic as well as about the estimate for the cost of construction, while the poor knowledge of the local geography shown by the scheme's engineer under cross-examination was damning. Objections were raised by local landowners, at least one declaring that he would not sell the land required except under a compulsory purchase order.

It was afternoon on the second day that evidence began relating to the narrow gauge project. Producing a plan, W. Forrester-Addie described the merits of the route to Welshpool and the advantages of the proposed gauge, mentioning the possibility of a later extension to Llanerfyl or beyond. Persuasive evidence followed from E. R. Calthrop, formerly engineer to the Barsi Light Railway in India, who indicated from his experience in that country that unmanned public level crossings need not present any danger. He neutralised objections to the necessity to transfer goods at Welshpool by advocating transporter wagons, a new and swift method of transhipment in use in India but, apart from successful tests by Liverpool Corporation, not then adopted in Britain.

Page 35 *UNDER THE GWR*

(above) *At Raven Square Halt in the 1920s. Note No 823,* Countess, *working bunker first to Llanfair;* (below) *near Castle Caereinion; the only overbridge, demolished by* GWR *in 1932*

WELSHPOOL GOODS
YARD

(right) *No 822 at water crane by the sheds;* (below) *view from south with closed cattle wagons at warehouse, 1956;* (bottom) *volunteers transfer ballast from* BR *wagons at Smithfield siding, 1962*

His transporter wagon for British railways, apparently, had a narrow body with a platform along each side beside the wheels grooved to take the wheels of standard gauge wagons which were moved on from a ramp-cum-stop block. Hinged flap plates between the side-platforms of each narrow gauge car were designed to allow a whole train of main line wagons to be run on or off at once.

More evidence, equally telling, was provided by Mr J. R. Dix, manager of the 2ft 3in gauge Corris Railway, who considered that even the trouble of conventional transhipment was a negligible price to pay for the advantages of narrow gauge. He had surveyed the district and come to the conclusion that a narrow gauge line would be able to cope adequately with the traffic, the natural outlet for which seemed to be Welshpool. A merchant from the latter town made a useful contribution by referring to a record he had taken of vehicles leaving Llanfair. The destination of the vast majority was Welshpool, he said, adding that coal and lime were costing as much as 10d (4p) per ton for carting from Welshpool to Llanfair. Messages of support were heard from others, including one from a Colonel Hughes who had been to the trouble of surveying the Meifod line. Evidence given in favour of the Welshpool scheme had been well marshalled (at no little expense) and scarcely any logical objections were raised.

With admirable speed, the commissioners reviewed the evidence presented at Llanfair Caereinion. On 4 September 1897, letters to the parties concerned informed them that:

with reference to the application made by Messrs William Addie, John Morris and others to the Light Railway Commissioners for an Order to authorise the proposed Welshpool and Llanfair Light Railway, I am directed to inform you, that after consideration, they have decided to submit in due course to the Board of Trade an Order authorising the line proposed.

Rejoicing at the news in Welshpool was accompanied by disappointment in Llanfair where, however, they were consoled by the knowledge that a railway to the town was at last decided on, even if their own scheme had failed.

THE LIGHT RAILWAY ORDER

Mr Forrester-Addie's committee members met once more on 10 March 1898, expressing their thanks for the energetic way he had steered the undertaking since its inception. They nominated the Company's first directors: this Board consisted of the Earl of Powis, Capt A. R. Pryce, R. C. Anwyl, J. C. Hilton and representing Welshpool Corporation—W. F. Addie, David Jones and W. A. Rogers. Frustratingly, two years were to drag by before the Light Railway Order became applicable. There were several reasons for this delay. The implications of the new Act of 1896 were still being unravelled, the draft Order submitted needed considerable amendment and negotiations were protracted regarding the company to work the line.

News came in January 1899 that HM Treasury had agreed to a free grant of £7,000 subject to certain conditions, including all the land needed being acquired for £3,000. At the same time the Light Railway Order had been issued by the Commissioners, but during the ensuing months there were still modifications to be made to it by the Board of Trade. The 56 sections of the draft Order had included provision for the company to deviate from the deposited plans as it saw fit (subject to Board of Trade approval), to construct a line of railway and sidings on the level over nine roads and to build bridges including an eight foot swing bridge over the canal in Welshpool. Powers would have been given to charge a maximum fare of 2d a mile for third class passengers, 3d for first class passengers and 6d (2½p) a mile for cattle, to run a workman's carriage once daily in each direction at a fare of 1d per mile and to convey mails.

When the Order was finally confirmed on 8 September 1899 it had 95 sections and two schedules and was the 56th to be confirmed. The powers of deviation were limited. The canal bridge was to be 'good and substantial' and clear of the water level by at least 7ft 6in, while power was specifically denied for use of the Order for the *compulsory* purchase of land belonging to the Shropshire Union Canal Company. A maximum speed limit of 20mph was now specified, further reduced on steep gradients, sharp curves, unfenced sections and road crossings. A maximum axle load of 8 tons was laid down. No less than sixteen clauses were devoted to provisions made for the use of electric power. The possibilities of electrification were currently being advocated—30 miles northward, the 3ft gauge Wrexham and Rhos electric tramway was completed early in 1903. Its opening ceremony was to coincide with that of the W & L. Beyond Welshpool, the Order required the provision of at least four fixed stations or stopping places with convenient approaches at which traffic of all kinds would be forwarded and received. These were near Castle Caereinion, Cyfronydd, Heniarth Gate and Llanfair Caereinion. All carriages had to have a 'proper and convenient means of access' if the company was to avoid the obligation to provide raised platforms. The maximum fare for all third class passengers was to be 1d per mile and no power was granted to carry mails.

Other requirements included signals where trains might cross (although no distant signal was necessary where the home was visible for a quarter of a mile), rail of at least $41\frac{1}{2}$ lb per yard, checkrails and metal ties on curves of *under* three chains radius and specifications for the securing of flat-bottom rail to the sleepers at joints. A turntable was not required, although the stipulation was added that engines running tender first were limited to 15mph. The compulsory purchase powers were valid for two years, while three years were allowed for completion of the construction of the Railway. None of the powers conferred by the Order came into force until the sum of £1,000 had been deposited with the Paymaster General.

NEGOTIATIONS AND PREPARATIONS

Almost from the time the Light Railway Commissioners' decision was announced, the W & L had been negotiating with the Cambrian Railways Company. It also made contact with the LNW and GW joint organisation responsible for the Welshpool—Shrewsbury railway and with the Shropshire Union Railways and Canal Company. The matters involved were the site of the actual terminus in Welshpool and facilities for interchange traffic—as well as the construction and working of the Light Railway. However, only the Cambrian was really interested in the new line. Though the agreement was bandied about for almost twelve months, the W & L had to accede to the Cambrian's insistence that the plans for the swing bridge over the Shropshire Union canal and for a siding to the canal should be scrapped, the clauses in the Light Railway Order amended and the line carried over the waterway at a higher level. Agreement was further delayed while the W & L secured an understanding that the Cambrian and not the Light Railway would accept liability for renewal of the rolling stock

On 6 March 1900 both parties were able to put their signatures to the agreement. Under the 99 year undertaking, the W & L would provide all necessary rolling stock as approved by the Cambrian while the main line company undertook to construct the line—within two years of the land being made available—and to maintain it. It was also to work the line at its own expense, and provide a 'reasonable and sufficient passenger and goods train service.' Of the gross receipts, 40 per cent were to be forwarded to the W & L.

During the negotiations, arrangements had also been made for Alfred J. Collin (Cambrian Railways' Chief Engineer, 1898–1901) to take charge of the engineering work at a fee equivalent to $5\frac{1}{2}$ per cent of the cost of the work. In other ways, things seemed to move slowly through the year 1900 as money was raised and as land was acquired—not without difficulty. When the Cambrian made a detailed estimate of the cost of the project, it totalled £43,204. The figure included £2,950 for the purchase of the land and buildings, £29,530 for the construction and materials and £8,100 for rolling stock. This was considerably more than had first been thought and the W & L immediately took steps to raise additional capital. The Treasury agreed to increase the free grant from £7,000 to £14,500. Local authorities were asked to increase their contributions and application was made for an amending Order. Issued a year later, the new Order increased the share capital to £12,000, borrowing powers were now £4,000 and, of the advances by local authorities, Montgomeryshire

County Council could provide £7,000, Welshpool Corporation £9,000, Llanfyllin RDC £2,600 and Forden RDC £750, while the Cambrian Railways' Company could subscribe up to £1,000. A mortgage could be raised up to £4,000.

Still costs rose and the flow of vital funds flagged. During the summer of 1902, a further approach was made to the Treasury asking for another increase in the grant to make up approximately half the anticipated short-fall of funds. For the second time, the request was speedily granted and the award of a new sum of £17,500 as a free grant was announced. But even with this increase in the grant, the Company's financial powers were to prove inadequate.

Previously, in December 1900, the Light Railway Company had had to review its plans in an attempt to cut its coat according to its cloth. First specifications included the provision of three locomotives, four coaches and a travelling crane. Despite the protests of Mr H. E. Jones (Cambrian Railways' locomotive superintendent, 1899–1918), whose company had to approve the choice of rolling stock, the W & L directors decided to cut out one engine, one passenger coach and a number of covered cattle trucks. Further savings were made by sacrificing the travelling crane.

When tenders were invited, the firm of Beyer Peacock of Gorton, Manchester, quoted £1,630 for each locomotive. Guest, Keen and Co of South Wales successfully quoted £5 1s 0d (£5.05) per ton for 800 tons of Bessemer steel rails, and the six tenders submitted for the civil engineering works ranged from £21,365 to £26,353. Additionally some permanent way materials and various buildings and other items were to be provided by local contractors. Several firms submitted tenders for the civil engineering works. Investigations into the standing of a Manchester firm, which submitted the lowest, proved it to be unsatisfactory. Of the others, the lowest was £24,290 tendered by John Strachan of Cardiff and it was this Welsh firm to which the contract was offered. After months of legal and other administrative effort, the time was near for work to begin on the ground.

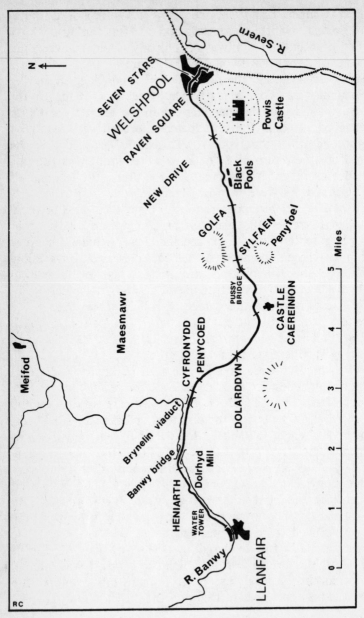

Route of the railway

CHAPTER THREE

Construction

BUILDING COMMENCES

John Strachan was offered the contract for the civil engineering works in April 1901. He not only accepted but, to the delight of the w & l Board, agreed to take part payment in shares. A contemporary issue of *Building News* recorded that this was the first contract to be let for a railway authorised by the Light Railways Act of 1896. Swifter progress at last became apparent. On Thursday, 30 May 1901, the first sod was cut in Welshpool with tremendous ceremony. The gaily decorated streets were lined with crowds as the official procession, headed by the band of the Montgomeryshire Imperial Yeomanry, set off from the Town Hall at 12.30pm. Not only railway officials and councillors were present, but Members of Parliament, the principal landowners, past mayors, magistrates, the police and the fire brigade! Turning into Colonel Hutchins' field adjoining Station Road, the dignitaries reached a beflagged grandstand erected by Mr Strachan. A burst of cheering from the crowd heralded the approach of a carriage drawn by a pair of superb bay horses and accompanied by outriders. From this alighted Viscount Clive together with his parents, the Earl and the Countess of Powis. w & l director, Mr J. C. Hilton, then stepped forward to present the Countess with an oak wheelbarrow adorned with silver mountings. While the band kept up a selection of choice airs, Mr Hilton turned to the young Lord Clive with an ornate spade (which still exists in the Powysland Museum, Welshpool). The silver spade had been inscribed:

Presented to the
Right Honourable The Viscount Clive
by the Directors & Shareholders of the
W & LLR COMPANY
on the occasion of this
Cutting the first sod
of that
Railway at Welshpool
May 30th 1901

Lord Clive dug the spade into the ground, cutting the letters
WLLR and removing the turf in the ceremonial wheelbarrow.
In a short speech which followed, the Earl spoke of how his
son would be reminded of the part he had taken 'in connection with the first light railway which had been undertaken

-꣠ Toasts. ꣠-

❀ ❀ ❀

	PROPOSER.		TO RESPOND.
	The Chairman.	The King, Queen and Royal Family.	....
	J. M. Dugdale, Esq.	The Navy, Army and Reserve Forces.	Major-Gen. The Hon. W. H. Herbert.
	A. C. Humphreys-Owen, Esq., M.P.	Success to the Welshpool and Llanfair Light Railway.	The Chairman.
	Thomas Watkin, Esq.	The Right Hon. The Viscount Clive.	The Chairman.
	R. C. Anwyl, Esq., D.L.	The Contributing Authorities.	The Ex-Mayor of Welshpool for the Welshpool Cor-poration. Captain Mytton for the Montgomery County Council.
	Lt.-Col. E. Pryce-Jones, M.P.	The Engineer and Contractor.	Mr. Collin, C.E. Mr. Strachan.

-꣠ Menu. ꣠-

❀ ❀ ❀

Salmon and Mayonaise.
Dressed Crabs.

Roast Lamb.   Ribs of Beef.
Farcied Chicken.   York Ham.
Pressed Beef à la Benoist.
Veal and Ham Pies.   Pigeon Pies.
Boiled Chicken.   Roast Chicken.
Tongue.
Ducklings.   Cream of Veal.
Croquettes of Foie. Gras.
Lobster Salad.

Wine Jellies.   Fruit Tarts.
Italian Creams.   Geneva Pastry.
Camerbert, Cream, Gorgonzola, & Cheddar
Cheese.

Menu for the official luncheon to celebrate the cutting of the first
sod, 30 May 1901

under the Light Railway Act.' Then the band led the procession back to the Town Hall for luncheon and more speech
making. A. C. Humphreys-Owen, MP and Chairman of the
Cambrian Railways, compared the earlier failure of private

enterprise to build a railway to Llanfair with the result of the united efforts of public bodies, rate-payers' representatives and private persons. A. J. Collin, the engineer, spoke of how they expected to complete the railway within a few months—in fact it was to take little short of two years. Lord Powis, applauding the generous terms the Cambrian Company had agreed to for running the line, predicted—more truly than he knew—that it would take more than that Company's 60 per cent share of the receipts to work the line.

This grand occasion was quickly followed by commencement of the construction work. Strachan's men began on Monday 2 June 1901, the third day after the sod-cutting, and a hundred men were soon engaged on the project. During the first few months work included the arching of the Lledan Brook in Welshpool and preparatory work for all the bridges and cattle creeps, the foundations being ready for all these by the end of July. When Welshpool Council complained about the risk of flooding arising from the way the Brook was being arched over in the town, the bridges in the Brook Street area had to be rebuilt. Nevertheless, the town section including the canal bridge was completed during the spring of that year, apart from the buildings. By now, half the formation of the whole line—and the fencing—had been done. For about a mile and a half out of Welshpool, the rails were in position and spiked down, though not yet ballasted, and a temporary line continued to Golfa to carry the contractor's materials forward. Beyond this point, earthworks were progressing at various points almost as far west as Cyfronydd and other work was going on still further up the valley.

DIFFICULTIES AND DELAYS

A start had been made on building the two main viaducts —the Brynelin viaduct over a ravine near Cyfronydd and the girder bridge to carry the line over the River Banwy on the approach to Heniarth station. Both gave trouble to the engineer. In August 1901, members of the Board of the W & L had toured the works in progress and after visiting the Banwy bridge works they had complained to the Cambrian Railways Company about the 'perishable nature' of the stone with which it was being built. As a result, A. J. Collin, the engineer, had agreed that it should be rebuilt with better stone. The erection of the bridge was finally completed during the following year, 1902, at a cost of £998.

Near Cyfronydd, the Cwmbaw stream occupied a deep, wooded defile just before it emerged to join the Banwy. Over this defile, the 32ft high Brynelin viaduct was being constructed of local stone. It was to have six 25ft arches. Difficulties were encountered in the making of the foundations and by the time they had been laid for six of the seven piers, a spell of cold weather (in February 1902) delayed the laying of masonry and concrete even further. By this time, £17,900 had been expended on payments to the contractor, on land purchase and other items. The time had now come to seek an instalment of the Treasury's free grant. Before the payment was made, the works in progress were inspected by Major Druitt from the Board of Trade's Railway Department with Forrester-Addie and Collin in attendance.. The inspector reported on the progress being made with satisfaction, and a cheque was forwarded to Welshpool for £7,250, half the total sum then promised.

Construction gangs generally worked ten hours a day and 'excavators' were usually paid 7d (3p) an hour, although less was paid for boys and a penny or two more for craftsmen such as stone-masons. While working on the line near Castle Caereinion in 1902, a number of them caused the village constable acute embarrassment by not only getting drunk but becoming aggressive and insulting and harrassing the inhabitants of the small hill-top village. Unfortunately, there was no cell in the village where they could be locked up. How they were eventually restrained is not recorded but soon afterwards they had to appear before the local magistrates and were duly fined. On an earlier occasion, in November 1901, their abundant energy and high spirits had been tapped to form a joint Welshpool and Llanfair and Tanat Valley Light Railway contractor's team for a rugby match against the Oswestry town team.

During the building of the railway, the contractor provided

the men with his own primitive rolling stock, typical of that commonly employed for such projects. Small 2ft 6in gauge locomotives were used. Until the permanent water tank at the Llanfair end was completed, a temporary tank was erected on the Banwy bridge, lifting its water from the river to service the contractor's diminutive locomotives. During the final stages of construction, the contractor hired *The Earl* (for £50) to haul trains conveying his men to work, its tractive effort being appreciated on the considerable gradients along the line. At Welshpool there was for a time a temporary standard gauge track. It ran through the site of the narrow gauge goods yard and here John Strachan had a standard gauge 4–coupled tank engine—*Strachan No. 3*.

Although at one time it was thought that the railway might be ready by August 1902, there was more trouble ahead and meanwhile costs were rising. Excavations were encountering rock unexpectedly and doubt about the accuracy of the surveyor's levels necessitated changes in the planned gradients. The engineer and contractor were having to execute considerable extra work at Heniarth to transform the narrow, twisting, steeply graded track from the main road into a satisfactory approach to the station. The necessity for widening, lowering and metalling this lane was to be contested later when the company and the contractor became involved in a lawsuit, but timber hauliers using the approach in later years were no doubt grateful for the improvements.

During the summer of 1902, it was necessary to apply to the Board of Trade for an extension of the time granted by the Light Railway Order for construction. It was agreed to extend the expiry of this period from September 1902 to 7 March 1903. This seemed more than adequate for, in the early autumn of 1902, the engineer considered that work was nearing completion and there was discussion of a formal opening date towards the end of November. But this was reckoning without the wiles of the local climate. To the consternation of the construction gangs, the end of 1902 brought almost continuous heavy rain, something for which this mountainous district tends to be notorious. This hampered work considerably and the *Border Counties Advertizer* reported that the opening would be delayed until the middle of December, although even this proved to be over-optimistic.

The wet weather caused slips in some of the cuttings, and these had to be cleared out, the slopes made flatter and extra drains inserted. Near Dolrhyd Mill, between Heniarth and Llanfair, the river rose in angry and menacing torrents and finally flowed over on to the line, washing away the new ballast and spoiling much of the work which had been done. Eventually, as the water receded, the river walls were built up an extra twelve inches to help prevent a recurrence of the disaster. In all, the inhospitable Welsh weather cost the Company many weeks delay and an extra £760 for the measures made necessary. Happily, the construction was eventually finished with a complete 'immunity from accidents' to the men, as the contractor afterwards remarked.

While construction workers were striving to complete the task in the face of these set-backs, another struggle was becoming serious. This was in the board room; how best could the now inadequate finances be eked out? In July 1902 the Board of Trade had announced the increase in the free grant (to £17,500), but even with this it was clear that the company would be short of the total capital required. Various attempts to raise more were made throughout the summer, including canvassing the residents of Welshpool.

One way of reducing capital costs was to eliminate the cost of signalling apparatus. It was at this time that the Cambrian Railways Company was persuaded to agree to work the line on a 'one engine in steam' basis. The Cambrian also agreed that plans for a locomotive shed at Llanfair could be dropped but not those for a carriage shed at Welshpool, though this was to be shortened to accommodate only two coaches. A suggestion to shorten the tranship shed at Welshpool was rejected by Denniss as it had to hold two Cambrian Railways wagons at once. The W & L Board was right to cut back in the circumstances. A hint of the future course of events might well have been seen, if it could have been appreciated, in the first public motor service between Llanfair and Welshpool which had started on 3 December 1900. Augmenting the existing horse-drawn omnibus, Tom Norton's covered wagonette ran twice daily in a journey time of 50

minutes—quicker then than the new train service when
that started.

The first vehicles ordered for the line were two six-wheeled
coupled tank engines. In March 1902, the Cambrian was explaining that building had been delayed as they had had to
be specially designed. In view of this, the W & L was considering hiring a locomotive from W. G. Bagnall and Co of
Stafford for the opening, but during August the first of their
own was completed. It arrived at the Cambrian Railways
station in Welshpool in September 1902, having been conveyed on what a contemporary newspaper called a 'special
trolley'. Transferred immediately to the metals of the new
railway, *The Earl* as it was destined to be, was temporarily
stowed under a tarpaulin. Three weeks later, the sister engine
set off from Beyer Peacock's Gorton works near Manchester,
being unloaded at Welshpool on 30 September 1902.

Well before the end of that year, the initial goods and
passenger vehicles had arrived from the Lanarkshire firm of
R. Y. Pickering and Co. For less than the cost of the two
locomotives, this firm provided three passenger coaches, forty
4-wheel open goods wagons and several vans, two of which
were for cattle. Generally, they were scaled down versions
of main line stock; the designs were drawn up by Herbert E.
Jones, the Cambrian's locomotive superintendent. Jones'
expertise in this matter was disputed by E. R. Calthrop, the
specialist on light railways who had spoken at the Inquiry in
1897 and currently engineer to the Leek & Manifold
Light Railway—also under construction. Calthrop believed
that long, steel-framed 8-wheel freight vehicles with a low
axle load and with his patent centre buffer coupling would
have been better for this gauge. He criticised cheap, heavy,
wooden framed wagons like those at Welshpool and he was
scornful of the choice of Norwegian hook couplings. He
referred to the excessive slack between the buffer heads and
to jamming which would occur when short and long vehicles,
coupled together, were hauled round curves.

But Herbert Jones' original designs had been worse. He had

planned unsprung wagons fitted with wooden block buffers. These rudimentary ideas had dismayed the wagon makers who had offered to provide sprung coupling devices at no increase on the £25 basic cost. They reminded Jones of the necessity of all the stock having identical fittings in view of the intention of running mixed trains. Built thus, the set of rolling stock was considered by Jones to be superior to that of other narrow gauge lines.

Nevertheless, difficulties were experienced with the new freight stock soon after its arrival. In November 1902, there was anxiety when couplings broke and Jones went out on to the nearly finished line to conduct tests. He reported that some wagons were coming loose, though he was not satisfied that they were being properly coupled together. The 'excessive gradients and curves' as he put it, called for extra precautions and so he advocated side chains with which all the stock had to be fitted by the time the line opened.

Even though the work was incomplete, no time was lost in making use of the new stock as soon as the permanent way reached Llanfair. On 30 September 1902, Strachan conveyed the first wagon of coal behind one of his little four-coupled locomotives and on 3 October, the directors of the W & L set out behind *The Earl*. Their accommodation consisted of seats in one of the open wagons. After some distance, *The Earl* was replaced by one of the contractor's much smaller machines, probably to facilitate progress over incompletely ballasted track. When the party eventually reached Llanfair, the event was celebrated with champagne before the somewhat precarious return journey began.

THE LINE DESCRIBED

In January 1903, A. J. Collin, the chief engineer, decided that the line was sufficiently complete for inspection by the

Board of Trade. This followed prodding by the w & l directors who had reminded Collin of the approach of the time limit set for construction.

There now existed a 2ft 6in gauge railway starting from a point in Welshpool's Smithfield Road and close to the Cambrian Railways' goods and passenger station (240ft above sea level). It was 9 miles 5 chains long, station to station; later spurs at Welshpool added another 7 chains of track. At this terminus, there was a gravel 'platform' and a waiting room with a booking office complete with awning. A short siding swung away into the Cambrian Railways' yard to the tranship shed, while the main line of the new narrow gauge construction curved off from Smithfield Road. Entering enclosed property, it passed the run round loop on the left and the three sidings on the right which formed single roads into the goods shed, the engine shed and the longer carriage shed adjoining. The Shropshire Union canal was crossed by a steel plate girder bridge with a single span of 33ft 4in. A siding to the canal suggested earlier but rejected in 1899 had eventually been agreed in July 1902, but was never constructed.

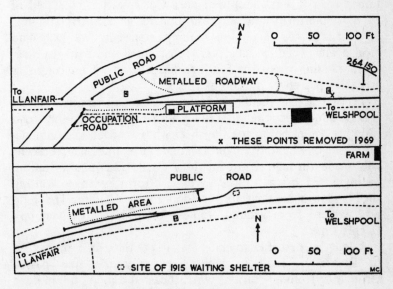

(*above*) Golfa 1903 (*below*) Sylfaen 1903

Crossing Church Street (later A483) on the level, the track dived through the newly opened gap between the buildings to reach the Lledan Brook. Above the watercourse, the rails were borne on longitudinal bearers supported by steel cross girders to enable the railway to reach and cross Union Street, where the Seven Stars Public House and adjoining Malthouse had had to be demolished and where trains would make a stop for passengers. Disappearing behind the cottages with two more stretches of viaduct, the route lay behind the Armoury to pass by the Standard granite quarry, where a siding was soon to be connected, and so to Raven Square. On the town side of the intersection, a line-side gravelled area marked the third station.

Gaining its own reservation again beyond the road crossing, and protected here as in most places westwards by a cattle guard, the line at first paralleled the main Dolgellau road. Later it swung away a little, to ease the gradient. Even so, it climbed at a nominal gradient of 1 in 30 for about a mile up the later renowned Golfa bank, with the track winding through some of the deepest cuttings on the line—up to 15ft deep. The ascent eased approaching a crossing over a minor road (Cwm Lane), and here Golfa station consisted of an 80ft 'platform' and a 120ft loop. Over the first summit, 603ft above sea level and coming alongside the Dolgellau road again, a siding had been constructed for Sylfaen Farm with standing room for four trucks. It was not envisaged as a regular passenger station at this stage.

Veering across the fields again, the second summit (578ft) was attained at the junction with another minor road (Coppice Lane) before passing beneath a wooden accommodation bridge—the only overbridge on the line. The descent was made through a cutting into Castle Caereinion station, distinguished by a 120ft gravel 'platform' with a waiting shed and a somewhat longer loop than at Golfa. The loop was worked from ground frames—there was no signal box at this time.

A lengthy descent, at first at 1 in 33, then at 1 in 51, led to Dolarddyn road crossing. Eventually the line passed through Cyfronydd station, which boasted a loop and another 80ft gravel platform replete with waiting shed. A little

Page 53 *LLANFAIR STATION*

(above) *Circa 1903. Note the low platform and the awning on the corrugated iron booking office;* (below)*in 1956 before demolition of the old van and coach bodies installed by the* GWR

Page 54 FREIGHT TRAINS

(above) *A once familiar duty. Over grass-grown track near Cyfronydd in 1962. The Earl cautiously heads into the Bawny valley with a load of coal in Pickering-built-wagons;* (below) *twenty years later, 0-6-2T Joan starts out from Welshpool (Raven Square). A train of ex-Bowaters, ex-Admiralty and ex-GWR stock replaces the wagons of sugar cane this locomotive hauled in Antigua*

further on, the Cwmbaw stream was crossed by the 50yd long six arch Brynelin viaduct, and a short descent at 1 in 25 brought the line close to the River Banwy. At about $7\frac{1}{2}$ miles from Welshpool, a girder bridge supported by two stone piers crossed the river on the skew in two spans of 32ft 9in and one of 34ft. Beyond this, Heniarth Gate station was built, having a shelter for passengers together with the usual 80ft gravelled alighting area and a 120ft loop siding.

Little over half a mile west of the station was situated Dolrhyd Corn Mill. The original plans were for the railway to pass along the slope between the Mill and the main road, but a last minute change of plan (which involved deviating beyond the limits agreed in the plans deposited with the authorities) saw the contractor squeeze the formation between the Mill and the river. This necessitated the remarkably sharp curves (3 chains radius) which are still a feature of this part of the line. On the west of the Mill, a water tower was constructed. It was fed by a ram, a device using the pressure of inflowing river water to lift water, at a rate of three gallons a minute, to the tank.

Following closely alongside the river, the railway ran past the timber yard of E. Jones and Sons (Tanllan corner) and then into Llanfair Caereinion station. The terminal was laid out with a 120ft gravel platform a few inches high, a loop and two sidings. On the platform stood the combined booking office and waiting room, wrought in corrugated iron with an awning projecting helpfully, while further along stood a urinal. The original goods shed was 30ft by 12ft.

Land for the line had been obtained from numerous owners, mostly in small parcels except for the three miles between the Armoury in Welshpool and a point near Sylfaen, all of which the Earl of Powis had owned. He had donated this land to the company, this and other gifts of land making up about half the total length and being valued at £2,400. The remainder of the land and buildings eventually cost £6,753—somewhat more than had been anticipated. Probably one of the most expensive single transactions had been the purchase for £1,175 of the Seven Stars public house in Welshpool. A troublesome acquisition was that of land below Golfa Hall which belonged to the Rev G. R. Pugh: the Order

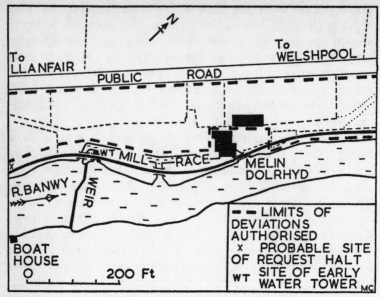

Squeezing past Dolrhyd Mill

specifically protected the reverend gentleman from compulsory purchase. When agreement with him seemed unattainable, Collin drew up plans to re-route the line. Clauses relating to this were drafted for inclusion in the Amendment Order 1901, but were repealed when agreement was at last reached in 1901.

The two major bridging works have already been mentioned. The line had also been carried over thirteen smaller underbridges, mainly over watercourses, and formed by timber baulks bearing each rail and mostly under 10ft 6in in span. In three locations, however, masonry was used to build arches to provide cattle creeps beneath the line.

BOARD OF TRADE INSPECTIONS

This was the new line of Light Railway which the Railway Department of the Board of Trade sent Major E. Druitt RE to inspect on Tuesday 3 February 1903. His examination was no less thorough than could reasonably be expected—including a careful survey of the ground frame equipment and rolling stock as well as the trackwork. The outcome was that he expressed dissatisfaction with a number of matters, although they were points which could readily be put right. Before the line could be opened, the inspector required check rails on all sharp curves on high banks and across the main bridges and steel ties on the sharp curves. He thought that in view of the 10ft fixed wheelbase of the locomotives, the gauge should be eased on the sharper curves by up to half an inch. Along the line, he recommended the fixing of mile and quarter mile posts, these increasing the construction costs by £36.

The ballast needed attention in places and the sidings at Sylfaen, Heniarth and Llanfair required slewing away from the main line to give more clearance opposite the trap points. He also considered that the centre buffer couplings on the rolling stock should have more lateral movement, otherwise they would be dangerous on the numerous curves. Below Golfa, the sharp reverse curves would have to be subject to a 5mph limit.

About two weeks later, on 20 February, Major Druitt paid a return visit. Many of the modifications he had asked for had been completed including the alterations to the couplings. Accompanied by the chief and resident engineers, W. F. Addie, H. E. Jones and C. P. Winnall (the w & l solicitor), he traversed the whole line in a train which was considered to be typical of the likely formation of an ordinary mixed train, consisting of a passenger coach, two covered vans, three open wagons and a brake van. It emerged that John Strachan's men had still more work to do. One of the results of the inspector's imposition of a 5mph speed limit on the Golfa bank curves was that alterations to the super-elevation of the track were required. Check rails at potential danger spots positioned 3in from the running rails, as he had suggested, now proved to be half an inch too far out as the wheels of the rolling stock were narrower than those of the engines and could possibly drop between the parallel rails on each side. Making out his second report, Major Druitt was cautious about certifying the line as safe and his recommendation that the line could open for passenger traffic was conditional.

This meant that the Board of Trade had still to await the

engineer's report that measures imposed with regard to the sharp curves were completed. The ground frames also had to be properly connected up and working was to be subject to an overall speed limit of 15mph (until the formation had consolidated). In addition, the Cambrian Railways Company had to formally apply for permission to run mixed trains.

THE OPENING IS SANCTIONED

Anticipating that these details would swiftly be attended to, the W & L board now made preparations for the long looked for opening. Provisionally, it was to be on Tuesday 31 March and, as the Earl was away in India, a telegram was dispatched to Bombay informing him of the imminence of the opening of the railway he had done so much to help, and asking him to return to preside at the ceremony. With little delay, the Board of Trade was able formally to agree that the line had been brought up to a satisfactory standard. On 4 March 1903, they wrote to Harrison and Winnall, the Company's solicitors, at Welshpool sanctioning the opening of the railway for passenger traffic.

Arrangements were quickly made to start running freight services. With the Chairman, the Earl, still on his way back from India, the ceremony marking the opening of passenger services was not expected before the last day of that month. On the Monday after the communication from the Board of Trade, 9 March 1903, Mr Price, the Welshpool stationmaster, supervised the making up of the first official freight train, fifty tons of grain and coal. Some unscheduled dispatch of freight to various points along the line had apparently already occurred, but nevertheless a small crowd—including Welshpool's town clerk—gathered in the yard to cheer away the train on this occasion. Starting away at 11.30am, it was *The Countess* which, with warning whistles, gamely hauled the load up the gradient through Welshpool's houses, fighting stretches of slippery rail as she continued.

Knots of spectators awaited the passing of the train at various points and the first stop—apart from road crossings— was made at Heniarth to detach a wagon of coal for someone in that neighbourhood. The train reached Llanfair station in just under an hour, to be heartily welcomed by a large crowd. Starting at 1.45pm, the return journey took little longer despite stopping at intermediate stations to pick up empties. A second trip was worked the same day and two more the next day—even before a proper advertisement had appeared in the local press. On 11 March and in several subsequent issues, the *Oswestry and Border Counties Advertizer* carried the following notice:

CAMBRIAN RAILWAYS

PUBLIC NOTICE

**THE LINE BETWEEN
WELSHPOOL AND LLANFAIR**

IS NOW OPEN

FOR
**GOODS, MINERAL AND LIVE STOCK
TRAFFIC**

RATES and other information may be obtained from the Company's Agents at Welshpool and Llanfair, or from Mr. W. H. GOUGH, Traffic Superintendent, Oswestry.

C. S. DENNISS,
Secretary and General Manager.
Oswestry, March, 1903.

Arrangements had to be finalised to start passenger services, and application was made to the Treasury for payment of the balance of the free grant. Bureaucracy now took a hand. Under an agreement made in 1901 with the Cambrian Railways and the W & L, the Treasury had undertaken to pay the second instalment of the free grant if the line should 'open within the time limited by the Order . . . . for public traffic'. Correspondence passed to and fro between HM Treasury and the Board of Trade while the meaning of 'public traffic' in the agreement was disputed. As long as the Board of Trade could only certify that the railway had opened for goods traffic, the Treasury was reluctant to part with the funds. It was decided to ask the W & L to render a statutory declaration from the working company that the line had actually been opened. With this, the Board of Trade's Railway Department felt able to issue certificate No R.3680 which, at last, the Treasury accepted as evidence that it could forward the £10,250 needed by the W & L. Signed by Sir Herbert Jekyll, assistant secretary to the Board of Trade, on 3 April 1903, the last paragraph read:

And whereas on the 4th day of March 1903, the Board of Trade, having considered the terms of the said report (viz. Major Druitt's) and being satisfied that the said Light Railway had been properly completed, sanctioned the use of the line for the public conveyance of passengers. Now therefore the Board of Trade do hereby certify that the Welshpool and Llanfair Light Railway has been completed to their satisfaction and is fit for public traffic.

Signed by Order of the Board of Trade, this 3rd day of April 1903.

Share certificate of the W & LLR, dated 31 October 1904

CHAPTER FOUR

The Cambrian Era

THE OPENING CEREMONY

Saturday 4 April 1903 was finally chosen as the day for the inauguration of passenger services. At Welshpool, the day brought with it cold and rainy conditions although these were ameliorated by the gay appearance of the town which was decorated with flags and coloured bunting. The Earl of Powis—the Chairman of the Company—directors W. Forrester-Addie and C. Shuker, together with Mr John Evans, the w & l secretary, met briefly to fix the Company's common seal to an agreement with the Cambrian that the line would be worked in accordance with Board of Trade requirements.

In Smithfield Road, the special train was drawn up with *The Countess* simmering at the head of the three bronze-green and white coaches. The engine, smartly painted in black and lined in orange yellow, was embellished for this occasion with green and red art muslin, red rosettes sporting yellow centres and the traditional daffodils. Displayed on the smokebox door and on the rear bunker panel were the Prince of Wales feathers surrounded by leeks, while white letters on a red background on the boiler side proclaimed 'Success to the w & llr'. Long before the fixed time for departure, groups of interested spectators had begun to assemble so that by eleven o'clock there was a gathering of several hundred people standing in the nearby road. A warm welcome was accorded the Earl of Powis when he drove up in his dogcart to be joined by his co-directors. In turn they welcomed the officials of the Cambrian Railways Company who alighted at the main line station from a special train from Oswestry.

Shortly after 11.15am, the signal was given for the train to start, with Herbert Jones, the Cambrian's locomotive superintendent on the footplate. Amid the cheering of the crowds along the route, the ringing of bells and a fusillade of detonators, the 'special' steamed forward through Welshpool town. At every vantage point the inhabitants gathered to give the 'little train' a hearty cheer and at the Standard Quarry rocks were blasted as it approached. Some guests arriving late from Shrewsbury made use of the 'bus from the Royal Oak Hotel to enable them to dash to Llanerchydol Gates (Raven Square) where the train made a brief stop to pick them up before setting out on the rural journey. At various points along the line, small groups of country folk had gathered and gave the 'special' a vociferous welcome. A stop was made at Cyfronydd, to entrain Captain Pryce, the company's deputy chairman who chose to start his ceremonial ride from the neighbourhood of his home.

A non-stop run brought the train to Llanfair terminus, passing first under a huge arch of greenery and then into the crowded station to the accompaniment of fog signals and sustained loud cheering. More evergreen arches had been erected near the entrance and the little station was decorated overall with flags and banners. It is recorded that even one of the Llanfair busmen, who expected to be superseded, paraded alongside in the road with his horse and vehicle decked out in ribbons and bright colours. The day was taken as a holiday in Llanfair; the church bells had been ringing all morning and the waiting villagers had been entertained by the Llanfair band. The passengers now alighted from the inaugural train and, from the waiting room, biscuits and jugsful of champagne were dispensed—supplied by the proprietor of Llanfair's Wynnstay Arms Hotel. These were the days when champagne cost 6s (30p) per bottle. Mr W. A. Jehu (whose land had been used for that end of the line) found a vantage point on a large boulder, and on behalf of the inhabitants of the district welcomed the new railway. The Earl replied, mentioning the near £50,000 spent and their inability to find funds to equip the line to run more than one engine in steam.

When it was time for the train to return, many of the

folks from Llanfair attempted to take advantage of the opportunity of having a free ride to Welshpool. The station-master, Mr Barrow-Griffiths, and his helpers had great difficulty in closing the gates of the new coaches. Thus it was a little past the scheduled departure time of 1.00pm when *The Countess* was able to pull out, reaching Seven Stars in Welshpool less than three quarters of an hour later. A large party alighted and repaired to the Royal Oak Hotel for luncheon—and more speechmaking. In final commemoration of the occasion, a medal was struck bearing the arms of the borough.

Medal struck to mark the opening of the railway

The opening of the line, sought after for so many years, had been celebrated in fine style, yet this did not stifle criticism from some of the populace. Keen to derive maximum benefit from the new railway—which many of them had wanted to come from Arddleen and Llanymynech—the inhabitants of Llanfair held public meetings during the first month of operation to convince the Cambrian that its freight rates were too high and its passenger timetable inconvenient and slow. Perhaps there was some substance in these complaints—the working company quickly made some reduction in its rates, although not enough to satisfy all its critics. Two years later it was able to lop a quarter of an hour off the journey time, reducing it to 55 minutes each way. Some of the people of Caereinion were disappointed that there were only three trains each day at first and that none arrived at Llanfair later than 6.05pm, but soon a later working was introduced.

After the opening of the w & l in 1903, passenger services

seem to have been almost unexpectedly well patronised, though mid-week services settled down to a steadier rhythm of traffic. The first Monday market trains were heavily laden with passengers, packed 'like sardines in a tin' according to a contemporary report. On at least one occasion, the services of the Welshpool Constabulary were required to keep order among the crowds wishing to return to Llanfair in the evening. The visit to Welshpool market had formerly been something of a special occasion, but now for many inhabitants of Llanfair Caereinion and its hinterland it became a regular habit. The up morning trains were packed, their passengers clutching baskets of cheese, butter, eggs and other produce. Frightened chickens and ducks stared down from the hampers in bewilderment as the carriages jolted and lurched. Stops at intermediate stations often occasioned a mad scramble to squeeze on to the already overcrowded coaches. Fortunately—for travellers—trains on most other days offered a rather pleasanter, less cramped journey.

Business in Welshpool improved, but somewhat paradoxically so did trade in Llanfair. The boom there was the result of the incursion into the little town of many farmers from the upper parts of the Banwy basin and from over the hill to the south—the folk of Cefn Coch and Adfa forsaking the trek down the Bechan valley. From Llanfair station was collected coal and lime which had previously been carted from Llanfyllin and Newtown. Llanfair Caereinion also hoped that its tourist trade would develop; it advocated its sulphur springs to health seekers and advertised the splendid scenery which now could be so easily reached. The Wynnstay Arms pronounced itself a 'First Class Hotel for Families, Tourists & Commercial Gentlemen', arranged for a conveyance to meet all trains and supplied its clientele with its noted home-brewed beer. Excursion facilities to Llanfair were offered from Cambrian Railways' stations and, in 1903, there were reports of a considerable influx of visitors on Saturdays. This perhaps accounted for numbers of would-be passengers being left behind in Welshpool by morning trains crammed to capacity.

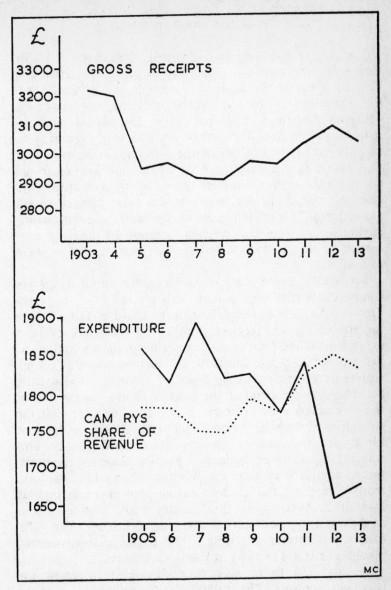

Receipts and expenditure to 1913

FINANCIAL DIFFICULTIES

The years ahead were to be marked by mediocracy rather than éclat. Shortage of capital was to prove restrictive and irksome. Even at the inaugural ceremony on 4 April 1903, the optimism customary in the speechmaking on such occasions had been tempered with mention of financial stringency. The cost of the ceremony itself had eventually to be paid out of the pockets of the directors of the w & l at £38 19s 9d (£38.99) per head. Not that these gentlemen did not make some efforts to raise more capital. Only three days after the official opening, a canvas was being planned to sell more shares. This brought some success and some outstanding creditors who were now charging interest on their accounts —such as Beyer Peacock and R. Y. Pickering & Co—were paid off.

But within a year—and with the contractor's bill not yet completely settled—application was necessary for an extra Treasury grant. It was explained to the Board of Trade, where the application was received, that £47,364 had already been expended but the total cost of the railway and its equipment had reached £56,945. Much of the balance was still owing. Letters from the Earl to the Board of Trade and a visit from Forrester-Addie convinced the Board's Grants Committee of the earnestness of their entreaty. It was made clear that the difficulties of the w & l were further complicated by the need for £3,600 additional to the amount of the deficiency. This was for signalling equipment, a passing place to allow the second engine to operate, the purchase of an additional locomotive, carriage and timber wagons and more sidings at Llanfair. In August 1904, the Treasury made its offer—a loan of £5,700 at 3¼ per cent to cover the deficiency. The company was no nearer to getting a third engine or implementing thoughts of trains crossing at Castle Caereinion.

In 1905, an Order was obtained which increased the borrowing powers. The capital finally authorised and the amount actually raised is tabulated:

	Authorised	Raised
Ordinary share capital	£12,000	£11,065
Loans or shares—local authorities	£19,350	£19,350
Free grant	£17,500	£17,500
Treasury loan	£5,700	£5,700
Mortgage (debentures)	£7,000	£3,000
Total	£61,550	£56,615

Despite H. E. Jones' one-time satisfaction with the rolling stock, the effect of financial constraint on what was ordered soon became apparent. Even before the line opened, concern had been growing locally as to the ability of the railway to cope with the expected traffic. It was strongly rumoured that timber longer than 30ft would not be carried—indeed, at that stage, a local timber merchant had been advised by Mr Denniss that no provision was being made at either terminal for loading and unloading such traffic. However, a couple of months after the opening ceremony it was agreed that suitable rolling stock for carrying long timber ought after all to be purchased. The order, for ten trucks, was finally placed at the end of that year. The W & L was dissuaded from ordering timber stock which was unsprung and poorly equipped but cheap. Savings of nearly £20 on each £44 truck could have been made in this way, but as a solution to its financial problems the W & L accepted an offer of a form of hire-purchase spread over a five year period. Some trial vehicles were to be dispatched in advance and during 1904 six of these arrived. Two years went by, the remaining timber bolsters were not delivered, finances did not improve and the remainder of the order was cancelled.

There were other monetary problems in 1904. Strachan, the contractor, was demanding settlement of his outstanding account. There was some dispute over his bill for extra work carried out during the construction, including that caused by flooding and the alterations required by Major Druitt. A. J. Collin as engineer would not recommend payment, and the company's solicitor pointed out that work had been done outside the contract for which sanction should have been obtained before starting. The contractor now sought to bring a legal action to recover his money, but by the end of 1904 the proceedings were stayed as the Cambrian asked for the case to go to arbitration. On 29 June 1905, the hearing opened before the arbitrator, Walter Armstrong, the engineer to the GWR. Twelve months later, Mr Armstrong announced his ruling. He awarded Strachan £2,565 with costs to be paid by the respondents. On top of all this, the W & L had £300 to find for the solicitors representing them at the hearing. In July 1906, the company paid off £1,200 of the award, 'and thereby prevented the issue of a writ' as the minutes recorded. But capital was still so desperately short that the Cambrian had to advance the balance.

TRAFFIC

Overall, traffic never exceeded expectations. Freight rates remained higher than the rates for conveyance by road, and the old donkey carts continued running for some time in competition. At the end of the first year, the W & L as owning company took £661 (less tax) from the gross receipts. This was swallowed up mainly by interest charges, and there was nothing left with which to pay dividends. As the years came and went, the company was in fact, never able to pay a dividend. At the end of 1903, after paying working expenses, the Cambrian Railways Company was faced with a loss on the line, although in ensuing years profits gradually improved. Results for most years up to 1922 came near to the estimate of annual traffic made before the line opened by C. S. Denniss, the Cambrian's general manager.

	Estimated	Actual receipts for	
		1905	1911
Passengers	£1250	£1365	£1226
Coal and minerals	£ 500	£ 631	£ 520
Other Goods	£1500	£ 735	£1016
Parcels	£ 150	£ 177	£ 182
Livestock	—	£ 10	£ 94
Total	£3405	£2918	£3046*
Working Expenses	£2043	£1859	£1835
Net revenue	£1362	£1062	£1211

* includes some miscellaneous receipts

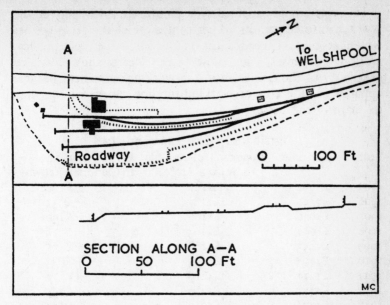

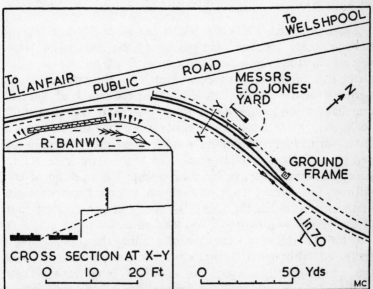

Handling the timber traffic (*above*) Scheme proposed for Llanfair yard, 1903 (*below*) Timber siding built at Tanllan Corner, Llanfair, 1904

This was not as satisfactory a picture as it looked, for the W & L had to be paid its 40 per cent share of the gross takings which at times exceeded the net revenue (i.e. receipts less working expenses). In those early years the acclaimed generosity of the Cambrian in the working agreement became apparent, as the cost of working the line came to more than its share of the takings.

Distribution of revenue 1905-13

Year	Net revenue	Proportion of receipts to W & L (40%)	Loss (−) or gain (+) to Cambrian Railways
1905	£1062	£1168	−£106
1906	£1156	£1187	−£ 31
1907	£1026	£1166	−£140
1908	£1091	£1163	−£ 72
1909	£1153	£1188	−£ 35
1910	£1198	£1195	+£ 3
1911	£1211	£1218	−£ 7
1912	£1431	£1236	+£195
1913	£1374	£1220	+£154

Detailed figures for a six-month period of 1906, a typical pre-war year, indicate that about 50,000 passengers were carried in the year, accounting—with parcels traffic—for about half of the total receipts. Freight in the twelve month period would have included about 3,500 tons of general merchandise and some 4,000 tons of mineral traffic (mainly coal), though the latter traffic made it a poor third in importance. Surprisingly perhaps, livestock accounted for only $1\frac{1}{2}$ per cent of total receipts—much of the livestock seems to have continued to move by road despite the opening of the railway. In February 1911, to facilitate attempts to take more of the sheep traffic, the Cambrian was asked to convert four of the goods wagons into livestock vehicles.

Before World War I the cost of running the line gradually decreased, although the engineer's account tended to swell the final figure. In 1909, for example, engineering costs totalled £521 as against £375 for coal (for 26,079 train miles) and £797 in respect of wages for traffic and locomotive staff. At Welshpool, two transhipping goods porters were employed for the narrow gauge traffic. More men were required at

WELSHPOOL SCENES

(top) *Where horses once hauled quarry tubs: moving the Society's newly acquired rolling stock in 1959;* (above) *the canal bridge; site of tramway wharf behind, on right. Lledan Brook beneath railings.* (left) **The Earl** *crosses Raven Square with enthusiasts in open wagons just prior to the closure by BR*

Page 72 *RE-OPENING DAYS*

(above) *On 16 May 1982, No 14 and* Joan *wait for the official guests after the Company's President, the Earl of Powis, had ceremonially declared the extension open;* (below) *re-opening day, 6 April 1963: through 'The Narrows' (now demolished) where the track ran over the brook*

Llanfair Caereinion where the staff included a stationmaster in the early years, as well as the booking porters and several goods porters. Other stations were unstaffed. Before World War I, the porters and porter-guards received 18s (90p) per week—or 10s (50p) if they were juniors. Wages escalated during the war and after, the same porters' weekly wages reaching £3 7s (£3.35) in 1921 before wage rates declined somewhat during the depression years.

ALTERATIONS AT THE TERMINI

The slenderness of the financial resources available for the building of the railway, and the resulting inadequacy of the yard accommodation at Llanfair Caereinion station, were referred to by the Cambrian's general manager on opening day. The following month, the works committee of the W & L considered suggestions from Mr Denniss sparked off by difficulties in dealing with the coal traffic. The committee consulted A. J. Collin who estimated that it would be possible for £200 to fill in the low lying part of the yard from the coal siding to the fence and lay in extra lengths of siding. Although it was agreed to ask the Cambrian to carry out the scheme, eight months later the expansion of facilities at Llanfair yard was still under discussion. Plans had been drawn up for the construction of an access road on the riverside of the yard as well as for lengthening the siding to which it would lead. But the scheme was deferred due to difficulties with regard to paying out John Strachan, the contractor.

A few weeks later, in April 1904, the construction of some additional facilities at Llanfair was agreed. These were to cope with timber traffic—the new bolsters had just arrived —and further plans had been produced for a relatively cheap scheme, not actually in the yard at the terminus but quarter of a mile to the east beside E. O. Jones' sawmill at Tanllan corner. By cutting away the bank on the curve, 90yds of siding were laid in, albeit inclined at the somewhat steep gradient of 1 in 70. These works were completed by the Cambrian Railways Company for £130. The W & L agreed it would contribute £60 when it was 'in a position to do so', and Jones & Son agreed to put up the remainder in return for a rebate of 3d per ton on their traffic. They had just purchased a large quantity of good timber which they were anxious to move.

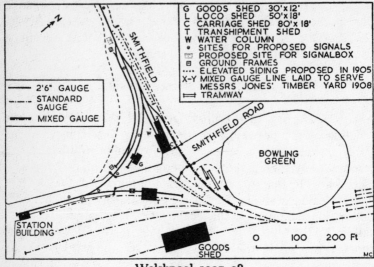

G GOODS SHED   30'x 12'
L LOCO SHED   50'x 18'
C CARRIAGE SHED 80'x 18'
T TRANSHIPMENT SHED
W WATER COLUMN
• SITES FOR PROPOSED SIGNALS
▥ PROPOSED SITE FOR SIGNALBOX
▣ GROUND FRAMES
···· ELEVATED SIDING PROPOSED IN 1905
X-Y MIXED GAUGE LINE LAID TO SERVE
       MESSRS JONES' TIMBER YARD 1908
⊨ TRAMWAY

——— 2'6" GAUGE
—·—·— STANDARD
           GAUGE
▬▬▬ MIXED GAUGE

SMITHFIELD

SMITHFIELD ROAD

BOWLING
GREEN

STATION
BUILDING

GOODS
SHED

0   100   200 Ft

MC

Welshpool 1903–08

The timber traffic included the handling of considerable lengths, loads up to 72ft long being carried. Timber trains were subject to an overall speed limit of 10mph. One contract secured in 1907 was for the conveyance of 50,000cu ft belonging to a Mr Barker of Shrewsbury. In connection with such traffic, the working company put in a cross-over from the W & L carriage shed road in Welshpool to the middle of the standard gauge Smithfield siding alongside. A third rail to give a mixed gauge section of track then led across the Smithfield Road to a stacking ground on the other side. The exact date of completion of this is not known, although an agreement had been approved in December 1908 between the W & L, Welshpool Corporation and the Cambrian Railways for the use of the siding—presumably for this traffic. Completion of this work must have inspired the idea of a reversing triangle. A peculiar system of moveable rails was installed in the Cambrian Railways' yard to link the Smithfield siding with the narrow gauge tranship siding when required.

Carriages (and very occasionally locomotives) were turned on this formation to even the wear on wheel flanges.

SIGNALS AT CASTLE CAEREINION

Along the line, a number of alterations were carried out in connection with the handling of timber traffic. The most important of these was at Castle Caereinion. In the spring of 1907, the Cambrian once again raised the idea of crossing trains here, using the second engine to head the separate trips necessary to work down the timber traffic. The W & L agreed to be responsible for the £190 bill and the operating company put in hand the work necessary to gain Board of Trade sanction for use of the loop to cross trains. Home and distant signals were installed and the opportunity was taken to construct a siding, presumably where wagons consigned to local people could stand without blocking the running lines.

Lt-Col E. Druitt—he had been promoted in 1904—came to inspect the installation for the Board of Trade. His report appears below:

> Railway Department
> Board of Trade
> 8 Richmond Terrace
> Whitehall
> London SW
> 15th June 1907

The Assistant Secretary
  Railway Dept.
    Board of Trade.

Sir,
  I have the honour to report for the information of the Board of Trade that in compliance with the instructions contained in your Minute of the 7th June, I have inspected the new works at Castle Caereinion on the Welshpool and Llanfair Light Railway worked by the Cambrian Railways.

  At this place a passing place has been laid down in the single line between Welshpool and Llanfair. A small signal box has been built containing 9 working levers and 1 spare lever. The interlocking and signalling arrangements are satisfactory.

This railway is a light one of 2ft 6in gauge and has hitherto been worked by one engine in steam but will be worked shortly on the Train staff and ticket system combined with the absolute block telegraph system. It is proposed to transmit the block signals by means of telephones at the three stations instead of by the usual block instruments.

I see no objection to this proposal but the Company should send a copy of the Regulations proposed to be used and also a fresh undertaking as to the mode of working signed by both owning and working Companies.

Subject to the above and to the new points and signals being correctly connected up, I can recommend the Board of Trade to sanction the use of the new works in question.

I have, etc,

(Sd.) E. Druitt

Lt Col RE

During November of that year, the new signal box was opened to allow a ballast train to work on the line simultaneously with the regular train. The box was closed again within five weeks and the months passed without the crossing place being used, as the W & L recorded in its minutes. Over two years after construction, the Cambrian agreed to reduce the interest rate on the W & L's debt for the new layout until such time as it should be brought into use.

Three years after Lt-Col Druitt's visit to Castle Caereinion, the Cambrian cut the number of trains and the hours worked by the men as it was now contended that the services were not being supported by sufficient usage. Even so, a day's working still required two shifts of men to work the trains, as the Cambrian's secretary noted critically. A third train crew to man the second engine in steam seems by that time to have been unlikely on financial grounds although, after the rifle range opened on Gwncefn, near Castle Caereinion village, opportunity for special trains needing the crossing facilities could be envisaged. But even for the opening ceremony of the range in April 1910, the inauguration party used the 11.45am service train. So the new signal box was left locked, opened normally only by the guards who always carried a key. They were able to operate the Phonophore instrument and the levers. By the early 1930s, the box is believed to

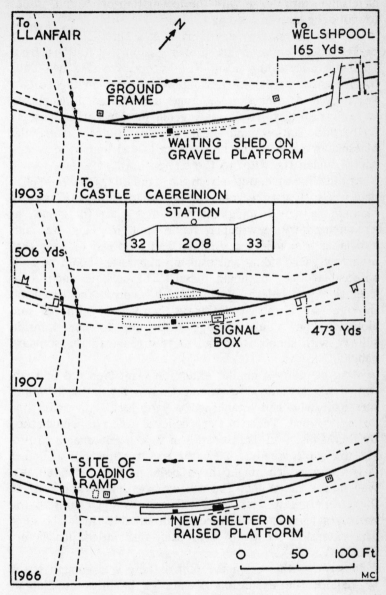

To
LLANFAIR

To
WELSHPOOL
165 Yds

GROUND
FRAME

WAITING SHED ON
GRAVEL PLATFORM

1903

To
CASTLE CAEREINION

STATION

32 | 208 | 33

506 Yds

M

SIGNAL
BOX

473 Yds

1907

SITE OF
LOADING
RAMP

NEW SHELTER ON
RAISED PLATFORM

O   50   100 Ft

1966

MC

Castle Caereinion

have fallen into disuse with the installation of ground frames to work the loop as a siding.

In 1909, alterations were made at Heniarth so that Mr Barker could transfer his timber loading operations from Tanllan corner siding, Llanfair. A sleeper crossing was built to give easier access to the loop which was lengthened two years later. At this time, a crane was located at Heniarth. Later, in 1913, a crane was erected for Mr Barkers' use at Cyfronydd station and quantities of timber from the Maesmawr estate to the north were loaded here. The W & L had to widen the gates to the station yard.

At the same time, traffic from the Standard Quarry in Welshpool was such as to warrant the Cambrian Railways Company planning 'a new loading and unloading place for stone', as a contemporary newspaper report put it. This was not altogether a new idea as Denniss had proposed in 1905 that a narrow gauge siding and tranship apparatus should be built adjacent to the Smithfield metals. The scheme under consideration just before World War I involved the extension through the Cambrian Railways' yard in Welshpool and alongside the standard gauge main line to new tranship sidings, with shoots from the narrow gauge to the standard gauge.

More plans for a similar extension were prepared in 1920, this time for unloading round timber for a local timber merchant who had established a yard beside the main line during the war. The plans are believed to have been backed by the Ministry of Transport. The W & L felt unable to provide the £140 asked of it for the construction, nor a further larger sum which might have been needed for additional wagons for the traffic. The scheme was left to the GWR to implement a few years later, adding about 4 chains to the narrow gauge system. Swindon built suitable timber bolsters. The extension seems to have been dismantled just before World War II.

In 1914, with war in the offing, there was enough traffic to require the expansion of storage facilities at Llanfair Caereinion station. Still poverty sticken, the W & L acceded to the Cambrian's demands but declared that payment would have to be by instalments—£50 down and £10 per annum for 10 years! By December 1915, the alterations had been carried out. Moving the western-most loop points towards the booking office had made it possible to enlarge the warehouse by 10ft in length. Siding accommodation beyond the loop was increased. It was hoped that this would make the handling of goods more convenient for customers and would encourage more traffic. Other measures which had been taken in an effort to expand business included suggesting to the Cambrian's traffic manager in February 1911 that he arrange the carriage of mails with the Postmaster General. It had been envisaged when the draft Light Railway Order was put together, but it was omitted from the Order which was authorised. The 1911 attempt was equally abortive.

PASSENGER FACILITIES

Two years before this, an additional halt had been agreed to at Dolrhyd Mill. Here Mr R. C. Anwyl, a director, wished to have a platform made and a hut erected at his own expense. A 'flag' station at this place had first been mooted in 1902 and used by Mr Anwyl's tenants, most of whom lived across the River Banwy. Parcels and papers were left here by the trains from Welshpool. A weir across the river maintained sufficient depth of water for a punt to be able to cross, the occupants hauling the craft across by means of a wire stretched from bank to bank. In December 1912, however, there was a calamity. Involved were a chauffeur and a serving maid who were intending to catch the train due out of Llanfair at 2.15pm. The surging, brown torrent, swollen by recent heavy rain and snow, seized the punt and hurled it over the weir, drowning the unfortunate couple.

At Dolarddyn level crossing, half a mile west of Castle Caereinion station, another stopping place had been advertised in the timetable since July 1904. (The Dolrhyd Mill halt was never shown.) Trains were scheduled to halt at Dolarddyn on Mondays only, though parties could make use of it on other days, everyone being charged to or from Cyfronydd and being issued with tickets accordingly.

Many travellers to or from Welshpool used the halt at Seven Stars in Brook Street. Surprisingly, no shelter there is recorded until the line had been working for nearly ten years. Then it cost the W & L £24 17s (£24.85). And it was even later, in 1915, that any shelter was provided for passen-

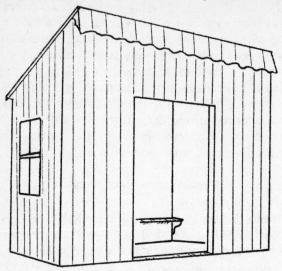

Waiting shelter at Sylfaen, built 1915

gers using Sylfaen halt, a bleak spot in winter. It had been decided late in 1904 to erect a waiting hut here, but the critical financial position at the time caused the erection to be deferred, although criticism continued in ensuing years from people who objected to waiting in the wet. At that time, there was not even a signboard here.

The coaches were illuminated by dim oil lamps. The Cambrian wanted the lighting modernised by replacing it with much brighter acetylene lamps used in their own main line coaching stock. With passenger traffic (at least) well up to expectations, there were accommodation difficulties. Even passengers travelling first class were grumbling about over-crowding at this time. The Cambrian therefore urged the W & L to provide a fourth coach, but the lack of resources inhibited the W & L from taking any action with regard either to the lighting or an additional coach.

Most services were operated by mixed trains, and it is said that the goods brake van coped with some of the overflow of passengers. The basic pattern of services up to the end of 1908 included four mixed trains each way on weekdays. No services ever ran on Sundays. On Mondays, Tuesdays and Wednesdays, an additional train, goods only, left Welshpool just after 5am, working back about 6.30am with a passenger coach attached. The first passengers could be conveyed out of Welshpool about 8.00am—the exact time varied slightly from year to year. The last train left Welshpool just after 7.00pm and the latest returning from Llanfair departed at 8.00pm (passenger only). No additional workings for freight were actually time tabled although some probably ran, notably those conveying timber.

During and after 1909, cuts were made affecting the first and last trains from Llanfair. Before the end of World War I, the evening passenger trains were discontinued completely, although in 1920 they were restored on certain days. But on Mondays, Thursdays and Fridays, people for Llanfair had to leave Welshpool no later than 3.50pm.

There were thoughts of connections westwards early in 1919 when the county council consulted Welshpool Town Council about suggestions for improving transport facilities in Montgomeryshire. The town council offered to support any

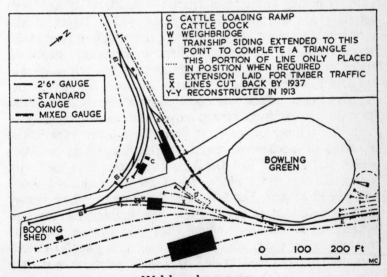

C CATTLE LOADING RAMP
D CATTLE DOCK
W WEIGHBRIDGE
T TRANSHIP SIDING EXTENDED TO THIS
   POINT TO COMPLETE A TRIANGLE
..... THIS PORTION OF LINE ONLY PLACED
   IN POSITION WHEN REQUIRED
E EXTENSION LAID FOR TIMBER TRAFFIC
X LINES CUT BACK BY 1937
Y-Y RECONSTRUCTED IN 1913

—— 2'6" GAUGE
----- STANDARD
   GAUGE
▬▬ MIXED GAUGE

BOWLING
GREEN

BOOKING
SHED

0   100   200 Ft

Welshpool 1913–37

scheme for the continuation of the Light Railway towards Llanerfyl and Garthbeibo. It also suggested a Light Railway— or alternatively a 'motor transport system'—to open up the New Mills and Tregynon area, south of Llanfair Caereinion.

Welshpool Town Council had been involved with the w & l more closely, a little earlier, in 1913. After some investigation it was decided to support the Cambrian Rail-Ways' Bill which would allow the line of Light Railway to be reconstructed near the passenger station in Welshpool. The Bill was also to authorise the third rail of the mixed gauge along the corporation's Smithfield siding from the connection with the narrow gauge yard eastwards. The Bill became law on 4 July 1913, giving the w & l running powers over the Smithfield siding backdated to 4 April 1913. For this, the Cambrian had to pay the corporation a small annual rent. Work commenced on 27 October 1913 and during the following week, passengers boarded and alighted by the locomotive shed. Staff were instructed to work freight to and from the tranship shed by means of the Smithfield siding and the temporary connection in the main line goods yard.

Welshpool Council welcomed the reconstruction of the passenger spur as it swung the railway inside the Cambrian's yard, removing the station from the roadway. It had been agitating for this for at least seven years. Trains at the terminus were now fenced off from the road and road traffic was unencumbered, except when arriving and departing trains crossed the road. A red lamp at the crossing was required to be lit during the hours that street lamps were on. A moveable stopblock was operated by a key to allow trains from the narrow gauge yard to move on to the road crossing.

In the summer of the next year, the railway experienced a period of mechanical crisis. On the first Friday in May, which was Llanfair Fair Day, the train came to a halt with a jerk on Brynelin viaduct. When the crew climbed down and peered beneath *The Earl*, they discovered to their dismay that an axle had snapped. There was nothing for the passengers to do but to complete their journeys on foot, and meanwhile No 1 struggled into the loop siding at Cyfronydd. Services later resumed hauled by *The Countess*. It was only three weeks later that No 2 was also in trouble. *The Countess* had hauled the early morning goods to Llanfair and was shunting the yard there when it became obvious that something was wrong. Examination showed that *The Countess* too, had broken an axle. Services had to be suspended, a breakdown gang was sent for and, while arrangements were made to convey passengers the length of the line by road vehicles, No 2 limped back to Welshpool. The problem was now acute as both locomotives were unfit for service. Not to be beaten, the Cambrian's fitters removed a set of serviceable wheels from *The Earl* and feverish activity saw them fitted to *The Countess* in time for her to resume work the next day.

A close-down, even for a short period, was to be avoided at this time as the railway was beginning to look more profitable. For the last two years, receipts had been greater than in any previous year while working expenses were about the lowest ever. Nevertheless, shortage of capital remained an embarrassment and even the regular income paid to the w & l automatically each year from revenue was barely adequate even to cover the interest on loans, let alone repay the principal or build up reserves. In 1914, local authorities which had made loans agreed to wait yet another seven years for repayment. Perhaps they had little choice.

PREPARATIONS FOR ABSORPTION

During the post-World War I period, the company had joined the Association of Smaller Railway Companies, the better to seek compensation for revenue which it was considered had been lost while subject to government control during and after the war. Claims became eligible under the Railways Act of 1921 and the w & l's case was based on losses from the arrest of traffic growth in progress in 1913 and income lost by the diversion of traffic from rail to road.

In July 1922, the w & l was awarded £2,667 7s—slightly more than anticipated and a useful contribution to the normally empty coffers. But at this time the directors were preoccupied with bigger things. For some months, negotiations had been going on with regard to the impending absorption of the w & l (and of course the Cambrian) by the

GWR under the Grouping of Railways Act of August 1921. The Earl of Powis and Major D. Davies MP represented the company in its attempt to arrange for the best possible financial terms. In June 1922, the Great Western offered £19,345, admitting that this was less than the full nominal amount of stock and loans. However, the W & L was not willing to accept this and four months later managed to wring better terms from Paddington.

The W & L got £23,236 in cash, including revenue and government compensation due to it up to the end of the year. The GWR agreed to take over rent charges and, in effect absolve the W & L from its remaining capital debt to the Cambrian which amounted to £2,387. Negotiations now started with debenture holders, local authorities and HM Treasury with regard to the repayment of what was due to them. Eventually it was agreed that the money would be allocated to the major lenders, as follows:

Debenture holders	90% of holding
HM Treasury (£5,700 loan)	81%
Local authorities	
(£14,625 in loans)	80%

Allowing a small sum for winding up expenses, this left ordinary shareholders with 4s 11d (24½p) per pound share. The last entry in the minute book of the W & LLR Company is dated 14 December 1922; from 1 January 1923, the company ceased to exist. After 23 years of nominally independent existence, the W & L and its foster-parent, the Cambrian were swallowed up by what became an even greater Great Western. Judged on actuarial principles, the flirtation with what was really a communal railway project had been a dear one for the locality: individually and communally they had lost about £14,000 of what they had put in (to say nothing of dividends forgone). It had also cost the exchequer £18,500.

CHAPTER FIVE

Under New Owners

GWR TRAINS AND BUSES TO LLANFAIR

When the GWR took over the W & L, there was a basic service of three mixed trains each way daily, and a fourth three times weekly. Extra workings were introduced on special days—for agricultural shows, fetes and so on. The Powys Provincial Eisteddfod at Llanfair on 16 June 1927 called for a service of seven trains in each direction, for example, and the last one returned to Welshpool half an hour after midnight. Sometimes the last trip out of Welshpool was worked by road motor bus. Typical examples of this practice were the late night connections put on from Welshpool to Llanfair for passengers returning from the circuses at Newtown on 5 and 12 March 1927.

In 1930, the cutting back of rail services began with the cessation of the thrice weekly working. For five years GWR petrol buses had been connecting Welshpool with Llanfair. Before the chocolate and cream painted buses were introduced on the Llanfair run, the GWR was already complaining of road competition in the area. The company realised that if it did not have its own motor service on the road to Llanfair, someone else would. Its road service started on 27 July 1925 and ran three times daily. It turned off the main road near Castle Caereinion and made for Llanfair over the hill road, one service continuing to Dinas Mawddy. Two GWR buses also started to run from Oswestry to Llanfair.

Perhaps the somewhat primitive single-decker vehicles proved unsuitable for the stiff ascents and dangerous descents between Castle Caereinion and Llanfair, for within five months they were following the main road, parallel to the railway all the way. It began to look more like sabotage of the company's own rail facilities, even though the bus services from Welshpool to Llanfair were soon reduced to two on most days. Four years later, however, the railway was closed to passenger traffic and six road services were necessary. The Great Western was no longer running the buses by then— the services had been taken over by the Western Transport Company, soon to be merged with Crosville Motors whose buses still serve the area.

FREIGHT TRAFFIC

In the twenties, traffic was, if anything, slightly greater than in the pre-World War I period. Passenger receipts were very similar and there was rather less coal carried but milk, timber and livestock had expanded. In 1925, a typical year, figures for freight carried were:

Coal and minerals	5639	tons
Goods	2579	tons
Milk	1368	cans
Livestock	344	trucks

East-bound freight included timber from Pen-y-coed (between Cyfronydd and Dolarddyn) for Messrs Boys and Boden's sawmills in Welshpool, and sheep and lambs to places such as Oswestry and Manchester. There were sheep trucks holding 25 and 32 beasts. A variety of materials was imported into the Banwy valley and, of course, the GWR quoted through rates inclusive of transhipping at Welshpool from standard to narrow gauge. Much grain and oilcake was carried from Chester and Ellesmere Port, iron and steel from Newport in South Wales and roadstone from the Standard Quarry. A great deal of basic slag came up the line from various places such as Aberdovey, Middlesbrough, Scunthorpe, Minera (North Wales) and Staffordshire. It was unloaded at all stations from Golfa onwards. Before the railway was built, farmers had required lime for their soils but basic slag had come to be preferred.

Wagons were apparently left in the loops for the customers to unload. It is said that when wagons of coal arrived

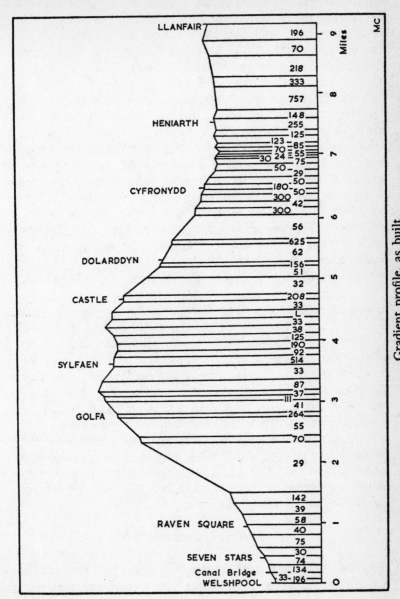

LLANFAIR — 196
70
218
333
757
HENIARTH — 148
255
125
123 — 85
70 — 55
30 24 — 75
50 — 29
50
CYFRONYDD — 180 — 50
300
300 — 42

56
625
DOLARDDYN — 62
156
51
32
CASTLE — 208
33
L
33
38
125
190
92
SYLFAEN — 514
33
87
37
III 41
GOLFA — 264
55
70
29
142
39
RAVEN SQUARE — 58
40
75
SEVEN STARS — 30
74
Canal Bridge — 134
WELSHPOOL 33 — 196

Miles
9
8
7
6
5
4
3
2
1
0
MC

Gradient profile, as built
Gradients can be contrasted with those of the planned profile

at Castle Caereinion delivery was announced to the probably distant owners by a recognised system of whistles sounded by the engine. When eventually emptied, the wagon was sometimes used—undoubtedly unofficially, as a means of transport to Llanfair. Castle Caereinion station is situated some 200ft above the river, alongside which the line runs to its western terminus and the descent commences with a 1 in 32 gradient. A 'good' wagon could be set rolling across the level crossing and then, with all aboard, would coast down Dolarddyn bank, pass Cyfronydd and even Heniarth before stopping near Dolrhyd Mill. Negotiating the road crossings must have been a hazardous business, nor were these the only danger spots. Regular train crews were used to this irregular practice and when they came up from Welshpool with the first train of the day and found the wagon gone from the loop siding, they knew to keep a sharp lookout for it on the line ahead. There was no telling where it would have come to rest!

On average, three loaded trucks or vans would be brought up the line by each train; two-thirds of those wagons hauled eastwards would be empty. Freight traffic brought in over £3,000 in 1925 and passenger fares added a further £1,200. 1924 was very similar. But this was insufficient. It fell short of the cost of maintenance, renewal and working expenses by some £2,000. Wages were rising—drivers at this time got about £4 10s (£4.50) per week—and working hours were being reduced, making more men necessary. The engines were uneconomical, partly because of the steep grades they had to tackle: coal consumption averaged about 7cwts for the return journey. Staff were being employed to work lighter loads than on an easier line, so that the cost of train running alone was more than twice as much per mile than the average for the whole system of the GWR.

PADDINGTON INVESTIGATES

Realising that some of its new acquisitions were turning out to be expensive liabilities, it was inevitable that Paddington headquarters should instigate an inquiry into the future of them. This is did as early as 1926 and the working

Page 89 *BANWY BRIDGE*

(above) *Newly-constructed, 1902: contractor's device for raising water for his engines visible on left and the locomotive* Strachan No 8 *in centre; (below) reconstruction by Royal Engineers in 1965. Massive jacks in use and damaged masonry removed to make way for new steel pier*

Page 90 *WORKING ON THE LINE*

(above) *The rebuilding of the line between Sylfaen and Welshpool eventually involved laying over 6000 imported hardwood sleepers. Castle station was the base where they were drilled for the railspikes; (below) No 11, the Hunslet diesel (now named* Ferret) *leaves Gofa siding with a permanent way train*

of the w & l was closely scrutinised. The terms of reference were not simply whether to keep it open or close it but whether more economical working was possible. The feasibility of replacing steam with a rail motor and trailer or even of removing the rails and converting it into a motor road was to be borne in mind!

The distance of the stations from the villages they served— though certainly not as great as some on other lines—was considered a handicap in the matter of attracting passengers. Furthermore, passengers on mixed trains were being delayed while freight stock was shunted. It was suggested that small goods which had to be transhipped could just as easily be transferred to a railway lorry and could be delivered direct. Though GWR lorries had not started running in this area in 1926, they were introduced within three years. It was not considered possible to reduce the running costs by replacing *The Earl* and *The Countess*—rail motors were unsuitable for the difficult inclines on the branch. In view of these findings and the deficit the line was sustaining, the report recommended closure. It was observed that under contemporary conditions, the w & l would never have been built. Had the recommendation been implemented, the railway would have been doomed after only 23 years' existence.

As Board of Trade permission would probably be a prerequisite of closure, an alternative was mooted. This was to restrict all activities to an eight hour span daily, using road motors for those passengers who must be conveyed outside these times. It was anticipated that this would avoid the employment of a second shift of men on the railway. Perhaps it was inevitable that a line that could only be built with a substantial 'social grant'—to adopt a modern term for the Treasury aid—would also need an annual subsidy for maintenance, akin to those awarded to certain of BR's unprofitable lines in recent years.

THE END OF PASSENGER SERVICES

Fortunately, however, Paddington dallied. Meanwhile, economic pressure was mounting and traffic on the line was diminishing. Though about eighty passengers used the train on market days, many other days saw trains running without a single passenger. Cheap returns (at the single fare), introduced to increase traffic, failed to do so and reduced passenger receipts by more than a third. Then, in January 1931, was announced, not closure—as recommended—but the withdrawal of passenger facilities. A notice appeared in the local press, applicable also to the standard gauge Kerry branch, and mentioning the Western Transport Company's 'compensatory' road passenger services to Llanfair.

It immediately caused an outcry. Welshpool Municipal Association quickly raised a petition; at Llanfair Caereinion, a special parish council meeting was hurriedly called and it drafted a protest letter to send to the railway company. They asked for an enquiry to be held at which they could state their views about the closure of passenger services and at which the company would have to prove the line's failure. It was stated that bus facilities were quite inadequate to deal with market traffic and bus fares were excessive. They made out a case of hardship that would be caused to farmers and smallholders in the Llanfair valley and suggested that there would be sufficient traffic on Mondays, Saturdays and special fair days to justify retention of passenger services on these days. Angrily they demanded to know why passengers could not still be carried on the goods workings which were to continue.

Soon afterwards, the Mayor of Welshpool met Mr H. Warwick, the GWR District Superintendent. Officials of the Municipal Association were also present. Mr Warwick laid some of the blame for the line's losses on the eight hour working day which necessitated the employment of two shifts of men. He mentioned the considerable saving which they expected if they reduced maintenance to the standards of a mineral line. The deputation's retort criticised the company's recent fare-cutting and a timetable was suggested for market days which the superintendent agreed could be worked by only one shift of men. He was persuaded to consult headquarters at Paddington.

Two weeks later, the parties met again only to hear that the GWR was adamant about its decision. The need for economy was over-riding and even the residents' suggested

Monday-only timetable was unacceptable as its last train from Welshpool at 1.00pm would suit only half the passengers. 'Either the number of passengers would be reduced from 100 to 50 each Monday, or it would be necessary to supply a second train and staff in the afternoon which would result in further loss', reported the district superintendent. Still dissatisfied, the Municipal Association afterwards stated that there was no provision in the Light Railways Act for closure, sought legal advice and, meanwhile, protested to the Ministry of Agriculture. Alas, it was to no avail.

At 4.00pm on Saturday, 7 February 1931, the last passenger train drew out of Welshpool station. It faltered up the incline to the town, then, with premonitory shrieks from the engine, wound its way through the alleyways pausing at Seven Stars halt for passengers to step up from the road. Some commiserated about the savings they had put into the railway years before—and lost. They didn't mind too much but they did not expect the line to close to the travelling public. So the train puffed manfully uphill with the solitary guard waving frantically in response to onlookers' sad stares of farewell. Even the GWR seemed reluctant to write 'finis' to the passenger services—for the coaches, removed to Swindon works, languished there for five years.

During the next 25 years, the Branch Lines Investigation Committee was to reconsider the fate of the W & L several times. Meanwhile the line was worked on most days by one trip each way leaving Welshpool at 11.00am and returning about 2.00pm. Trains, each with a brake van, were made up in accordance with the following limitations:

Coal and minerals	Maximum 7 wagons
General merchandise	Maximum 11 wagons or vans
Empties	Maximum 14 wagons and vans

Some of the staff were transferred in 1931 to duties on other parts of the former Cambrian system. There was no need for two shifts of crew-men any more; in previous years work had even started as early as 4.00am to prepare for the 8.00am departure from Welshpool. Steam raising was a long process—sometimes drawn out for as much as eight hours if the engine had been spare for some time—but it was much improved after the GWR fitted new boilers in 1929. Men from the former Cambrian Works at Oswestry arrived in that year to load the locomotives, in turn, on to flat wagons. On their return, 'westernised', they were more popular with the crews.

MAINTENANCE OF THE LINE

Maintenance gangs were also reduced after the end of passenger traffic. Whereas two gangs of four men had been responsible for each of the two sections, split at Castle Caereinion, one gang was given charge of the whole line. For the first time, men were given a trolley—a four seater with engine under the seat. They started work at 7.00am and finished at 5.00pm. Maintenance included patching the permanent way, two or three sleepers at a time, repairing the wire fencing (especially in spring with the birth of the ubiquitous lambs) and mowing the line-side grass by scythe each summer. The hay eventually went to feed railway horses. Major ballasting operations were restricted to Sundays and ash used for cheapness. Another economy introduced by the GWR was the practice of cutting main-line sleepers in half for use on the line.

A recurrent headache during the summer months was the creeping and bending of the track, and in an attempt to forestall this a great deal of time was spent oiling the fish-plates and also taking up the expansion gaps to pull the rails uphill. Even so, instances still occurred where it was necessary to remove or shorten rails and the gangs always had to be prepared to restore the lengths when the colder weather returned. One of the most troublesome stretches was the long straight east of Sylfaen. On occasions, the trolley was called out with crowbars to slew back the track snaking from ditch to ditch while the train from Llanfair waited until it was safe enough to pass. Several lengths at this point were eventually relaid with heavier rail.

The GWR Divisional Engineer examined the bridges on the line periodically through the thirties. During this period no repairs were ever required on the stone Brynelin viaduct (except painting the handrails), though on the 114ft long viaduct over the shifting River Banwy decaying transverse timbers had had to be renewed in 1929. It was estimated that the whole structure would require rebuilding in the year 2050! East of Castle station, a wooden overbridge spanned the track where it curves through the cutting. It had been erected to placate the owner of the fields which had been severed by the building of the line. In 1932, the GWR decided to dismantle the structure and, at first, planned to replace it with a steel girder span. When the lineside landowner refused to contribute towards the cost, he was left instead with an accommodation crossing at the east end of the cutting.

COMPETITION

The GWR was quite worried about the activities of local road hauliers who were emerging and extending their activities now that motor lorries were becoming more reliable. In the early thirties there were no less than nine carriers at Welshpool and one each at Llanfair Caereinion, Chirbury and the more distant Aberystwyth. The GWR classed half of these firms as 'anti-railway' and noted those which received nothing by rail. When the opportunity occurred, the railway authorities opposed applications made by the road hauliers for extensions of their licences. A special watch was kept on a carrier based at Llanfair Caereinion as the firm was considered to be hauling traffic abstracted from the railway. Basic slag and manure from North Wales were being carried direct to the farmers—no more unloading at the stations and carting home as with rail-borne deliveries. Sheep were taken to Welshpool and Oswestry markets on Mondays and Wednesdays and, in season, to Birmingham.

Meanwhile, the GWR went on into ways of attracting—or retaining—rail-borne traffic. From 1936, private wagon users on the standard gauge no longer had to pay for the hire of narrow gauge wagons from Welshpool to Llanfair. This did not apply to collieries. The 10d per ton charge for transhipment at Welshpool was retained, however, despite concern at its effect. To help secure a greater share of the livestock traffic, loading facilities were installed at Cyfronydd station late in 1937. Cattle loading docks were also used at Llanfair and Castle stations, as well as in Welshpool yard. Covered storage facilities at Llanfair included the former waiting room as well as the warehouse and, in 1938, they were augmented by the building of a galvanised store shed. The awning of the old waiting room-cum-booking office, and two lamps, were removed to allow small lorries to traverse the one-time 'platform' to collect sacks of meal.

WORLD WAR II

On the roads, motor lorries were making plain the little railway's disadvantages, but the course that world events now took staved off the final reckoning. The 1939–45 World War brought a scarcity of fuel for road vehicles and exhortations to farmers to produce as much as they could to feed the nation. By 1942, two trains were running each Monday. A livestock working came down from Llanfair at 9.00am and returned with animals from Welshpool Smithfield market at 4.00pm. In September—the sheep 'season'—up to five trips per day were not unknown with the wagons and vans crammed, the doors of the latter vehicles having to be left ajar to provide adequate ventilation. At Welshpool, the beasts were unloaded in the narrow gauge yard and driven across the Smithfield Road to the transhipment pens—the mixed gauge connection had been severed for some years. The driving of animals along the road from the Llanfair valley to Welshpool was now much rarer than it had been before the war.

Once developed, the livestock traffic continued even after the end of the war. In one week in October 1946, for example, 530 sheep were carried from Llanfair destined for Macclesfield, New Mills and Manchester. At the beginning of December 1947, as well as 20 cattle consigned to Hanley, Staffordshire, there were 500 sheep for various Midland towns. Increasing traffic in feeding stuffs taxed storage space at Llanfair station and once again facilities had to be expanded. Condemned pre 1900 standard gauge coach bodies were brought by road for this purpose and installed along the northern side of the station, the first arriving in February

1940 and another and a van body during the ensuing war years. As so many able-bodied men were required in the armed services, the traffic generated by the war was kept flowing with the aid of female track workers. Two women worked in a gang with two men. Equipped with a motor trolley, they maintained the full length of the railway.

Though busier than for many years, it was not always possible to overcome the wiles of the notorious Montgomeryshire winters which had caused so much trouble during the building of the line. In severe cold spells, watering the engines could be difficult. The water tower near Llanfair was replenished by the use of a handpump which lifted water from the river but sometimes the Banwy was known to freeze over. On these occasions, wily crews ingeniously nursed their engines until they reached a stream bridge near Sylfaen which, experience taught them, was sufficiently fast flowing to avoid freezing over. It was not the pleasantest of jobs, even for dedicated enginemen, to raise the amount of water required by the bucketful from beneath the underbridge to the opening on the top of the tank.

Despite such resourcefulness, the weather managed to get the upper hand in the winters of 1940 and 1947 when coal lay frozen beneath a deep mantle of snow and prevented services for weeks at a time. Floods were another hazard. There were occasions when the river rose to cover the track west of Heniarth. Part of the bank was washed away following one storm just after the war. It may have been the same violent storm which seriously damaged the masonry of an underbridge down Golfa bank. It had to be replaced with a 'temporary' wooden structure which still survives some twenty years later.

By contrast, summertime on the line could be delightful. Crews had time to stop to collect sticks for the peas and beans on their allotments at home and, as the season advanced, their halts were prolonged to enable them to gather the hazel nuts and ripe blackberries which hung in profusion at numerous favoured spots along the line. Small wonder that it was known among railwaymen as 'the holiday line'.

PRELUDE TO CLOSURE

Nationalisation from 1 January 1948 seemed to have little noticeable effect on the running of the line. At the time of the changeover, British Railways proclaimed in the *Montgomeryshire Express* that they would 'do their best to preserve the fine traditions they inherit and . . . to provide a standard of service worthy of the rising national effort'.

During the fifties, at about 11.30am on most days, a train of about six wagons left Welshpool for Llanfair, astonishing an ever-growing stream of motorists when the locomotive emerged to cross Church Street. Trains were nearly always subjected to delays on reaching Union Street—where the Seven Stars halt had once been—while attempts were made to clear parked cars from the metals. About 100 tons of freight each week were conveyed westwards—perhaps half that of the line's heyday in the Cambrian era—and while coal and coke continued to form the mainstay of the traffic, trains often included the odd wagon of basic slag, bricks or cement. Agricultural implements, meal and oats also were carried from time to time, but general merchandise was now only handled at infrequent intervals. The collection of stone from the Standard Quarry had long since ceased. In 1939 the quarry closed.

The trains which drew out of Llanfair yard now usually consisted of empties. Perhaps once or twice a week, there would be a wagon of wool or bundles of empty sacks. Occasionally traffic was forwarded from or received at Castle Caereinion and Heniarth, but only rarely did it make a complete wagon load.

THE END IS NEAR

Even without competition from speedier and more convenient motor transport, it seems inevitable that the railway could not have developed as the thriving economic proposition it was once hoped it would be. The diminishing number of inhabitants in the rural districts that it served increasingly became a problem of widespread concern. Since the middle of the last century, the population of Llanfair Caereinion has halved. The process accelerated notably after the early 1930s. Well over half the local populace was engaged in farming—a higher proportion than elsewhere in England and Wales — and more modern agricultural techniques together with a desire, especially among the younger inhabitants, for less isolation from social and public services, was leading to a marked migratory movement out of the hill country.

The future of the W & L became more and more uncertain. In 1947, with closure under consideration but still not decided on, costly locomotive repairs could no longer be postponed. Execution was stayed to get some return for this expenditure, but in the summer of 1950, British Railways—nearly three years old and becoming increasingly sensitive to the unprofitability of the W & L—was again actively considering closing it. The divisional superintendent traffic manager from Oswestry informed Welshpool Town Council that alternative road transport arrangements would be made. The reception this suggestion met with was mixed. Some members of the council regarded the railway as a continuing nuisance. Others, however, gained sufficient support to secure approval of a motion asking BR to reconsider the matter. A few weeks later the district traffic superintendent met council delegates. After he had explained the Railway Executive's case, the delegates returned to the council which now took the view that no further action could be taken.

Early in 1951, representatives of the parish councils along the line deplored the proposed closure but showed less militancy of opposition than Welshpool Council. Surprisingly, closure did not come—there were rumours of strings pulled in high places—and in 1952 a Western Region spokesman denied that any decision had been taken to close, although he admitted that it was under consideration. This statement was in response to an enquiry from Eric G. Cope, a founder secretary of the Narrow Gauge Railway Society, who was now initiating a move to take over and preserve the W & L. Having been informed that, if it did close, BR would not object to selling the line and, inspired by the efforts of the Talyllyn Railway Society at Towyn, Mr Cope suggested either a national appeal or a private company to save the

W & L. He communicated with the Welshpool Town Council seeking help. However, the council would have none of this, having now made its own plans for building a car park and for widening roads where the line ran. Some support was voiced for the project if a terminal could be provided near Raven Square—shades of things to come, ten years later!

Some consignees were complaining of delays and damage to their goods. The stationmaster at Welshpool explained to his superiors that the rolling stock was 'of poor and old quality', while the traders agitated for delivery by lorry from Welshpool and threatened to transfer their business to road hauliers. Meanwhile, trains continued to run and their occasional clatter through the back streets of the town chattered defiance at those who wished to be rid of something which was nothing if not a local institution. But when both locomotives needed urgent repairs, no trains ran for several weeks. With the lifting of some narrow gauge sidings at Welshpool, the inevitable was heralded. Early in 1956 *The Countess* was removed to Oswestry Works and closure again seemed imminent. Various railway societies arranged trips over the line for enthusiasts who sat in open wagons and, finally, the announcement was made by British Railways (Western Region) that 'on and from 5 November 1956, the freight train service between Welshpool and Llanfair Caereinion will be withdrawn and the line closed for all purposes'.

SAYING GOODBYE

During the last month of operation, the now doomed freight trains conveyed 117 wagon-loads to Llanfair. The last goods working on 2 November consisted of five wagons of coal, while the previous day six wagons of coal, one of sheep racks and one of general 'goods' had been hauled up the line.

Towards the end of October, the Festiniog Railway Society organised a farewell trip on the railway for its members and expressed an interest in acquiring some mementoes such as a few of the couplings and, possibly, even the rail when lifted. Disposal of *The Earl* was still to be settled—there were suggestions that it might be sent to the Narrow Gauge Museum at Towyn—while about forty wagons and vans were to be made available to the demolition contractor. The engine made a brave show as it stormed out of the Welshpool terminus with the FRS 'last' trip. Rumbling through the town, the customary stops were made at Church Street, Union Street and Raven Square for the fireman to dismount and signal the train across as he displayed his red flag.

Up Golfa bank, watched by the inspector accompanying the trip, 16 year old fireman Ted Williams had to work hard as the engine poked its way undaunted along the twisting, climbing line. Across the deepening valley, the tints of autumn made an impressive display among the trees on the hillside. With a stop at Castle Caereinion where a traction engine was rusting beside the line, they reached Llanfair terminus with an hour to spare before the return started. From Heniarth, the train was followed by the motor trolley conveying the gang which had been dismantling the long disused waiting shelter there. Gaining the lower end of the line with a mile to go through the town, the Mayor of Welshpool took over the controls, guiding the 'Llanfair Jinny', as it was affectionately known, on its sad journey to the terminus.

FINALE

During the last week of scheduled operations, the small guard's van on the freight trains pulling out of Welshpool was crammed with passengers who had asked for a last ride to Llanfair. Some were local people recalling the days of the passenger services, some were staff from the main-line station and a number were enthusiasts. The privilege of performing the last rites, however, fell to the Stephenson Locomotive Society on Saturday, 3 November 1956. The train of nine wagons and two brake vans was equipped with seats 'borrowed', once again, from the platforms of the mainline station. In the yard across the road from the terminus, some of the W & L cattle trucks were being dismantled while, significantly, a sleek maroon and cream cattle lorry stood beside them. The journey was described in the *Railway Magazine* of January 1957:

The co-operation of the Western Region of British Railways was secured for the issue of specially-printed tickets and in the recovery of one of the nameplates of *The Earl* which was attached to locomotive No 822. The Newtown Silver Band was present and played at Welshpool and Llanfair and intermediate points.

There were 120 members of the society on the train of open wagons and many more were unable to attend because accommodation was strictly limited. Considerable local interest was aroused. Some of the houses adjoining the line in Welshpool and particularly those in the new housing estate through which it runs, bore decorations which suggested a Royal visit to the narrow-gauge railway.

The train started from Welshpool at 2.30pm and the occupants of a large number of cars vied with each other for vantage points on the way to Llanfair to secure photographs. At Castle Caereinion, official photographs were taken of invited guests.

The special returned from Llanfair at 4pm to the accompaniment of cheering crowds, the music of the band, and continuous whistling of *The Earl*. The latter's efforts became even more effective from Raven Square (on the outskirts of Welshpool) to the main-line station, and few residents could have failed to hear it. The climax was reached as the train approached the station where a '2200' class o-6-o and a 'Manor' 4-6-o joined in with gusto on their whistles till the train drew to a halt. Then the stillness descended, and only the band playing Handel's Funeral March could be heard—a fitting ending. On any standards, no branch line could have had its last day commemorated more tangibly or with more appropriate ceremony.

CHAPTER SIX

New Lease of Life

THE SOCIETY

When the take-over of the w & l was first mooted, in 1952, the idea of acquiring and resuscitating a doomed railway was quite new. The only attempt then working was that of the Talyllyn Railway Society at Towyn on the west coast—and that venture was but two years old. The Narrow Gauge Railway Society's inquiries regarding the w & l led to nothing, although negotiations throughout July, August and September of 1952 indicated an initial willingness on the part of the British Transport Commission to be co-operative. Representatives of the NGRS had got so far as discussing a tentative four figure price for the line and the stock. Details of running and maintenance expenses had been given to them too. Perhaps it was the suggestion that these expenses could reach £3,500 per year that caused the NGRS to inform British Railways that, in the event of closure, their interest would be confined to purchasing the two locomotives for preservation, preferably in Welshpool yard. Had closure come at that time it seems doubtful whether the line itself would have been saved.

When the end finally came, in 1956, the Talyllyn Railway scheme was meeting with success and the Festiniog Railway had been taken over two years previously. Prospects at Portmadoc looked promising. Such hope and enthusiasm was infectious and encouraged new interest in saving the line at Welshpool. A letter to the *Railway World* magazine in 1955 had suggested a scheme for a non-profit-making society involving diesel passenger services to serve the town section. Although nothing came of this immediately, it showed how interest was stirring. A fine photograph appeared in the

Observer in the spring of the next year and in July the
Llanfair Parish Council invited inquiries from railway enthusiasts who might be interested in taking the railway over
as a private enterprise on the lines of the Talyllyn Railway
Society. Special excursions along the line throughout the
summer, with passengers carried in open wagons, fanned
interest and a Welshpool and Llanfair Railway section of the
Branch Line Society sprang up.

Hard on the heels of this came news of another scheme.
During August 1956, William Morris, a London printer, was
busy trying to initiate a society expressly for the preservation
of the railway and he began making contact with British
Railways. Preceded by a letter to the *Railway Magazine* to
mobilise support, William Morris organised a special trip
over the line. It attracted about seventy enthusiasts who
were carried in four drop-sided freight wagons after handing
over the usual signed indemnities to the Welshpool station
staff.

The date was 15 September 1956 and it was a significant
day for the railway. Following the exhilarating ride up the
Banwy valley and back, a historic meeting was held in the
narrow gauge yard at Welshpool. Addressing the gathering,
William Morris outlined his ideas for saving the line. Many
of those present accepted his invitation to pay a subscription
and become members of a new society to achieve the objec-
tives Morris had referred to. The Branch Line Society's W & L
section also canvassed for members on this occasion without
much support. Within the next few months their organisation
petered out, while the society founded by Morris held its first
general meeting in London on Friday, 23 November 1956,
approving a brief constitution and electing its committee
including William Morris as secretary and Stanley H. Keyse
as legal advisor.

They were pioneers more truly than they knew. The
situation at Welshpool was not directly comparable with the
two earlier preservation schemes at Towyn and Portmadoc.
It was the first attempt to rescue a railway owned by British
Railways, and formidable financial and legal problems presented themselves.

While British Railways awaited an offer for the line from

the newly established society, the first news sheet appeared
and the first public meeting was held in May 1957 in the
Fred Tallant Hall near Euston, London, to augment support.
About this time, the possibility of leasing the line (instead of
buying) was mentioned for the first time.   Meanwhile, the
clerk to Llanfair Parish Council was reported to be activating
local interest, but at Welshpool strong objections were being
raised to the town section remaining in use, presaging a
truncating of the line which was to rankle deeply. The dis-
quieting news from Welshpool was shortly followed by an
intimation from British Railways that the transfer they were
now willing to negotiate would be limited to the section west
of Raven Square. Furthermore, on 7 May 1958, locomotive
No 822 *The Earl* was removed from Welshpool—albeit to
better cover at Oswestry Works—while membership had only
risen to 200 and hoped-for local financial help had not
materialised. The outlook was disconcerting.

Other factors, too, militated against success. The society of
those early days seemed to lack sufficient officials with
maturity and expertise. But somehow, the committee's
admirable enthusiasm kept things together when progress
was minimal and membership numbers were growing at
snail's pace. It is sad that so few people came forward who
were talented and experienced in the organising of such a
movement as had been formed, nor did the society attract
wealthy and generous well-wishers on the scale that some
similar projects have. These troubles have tended to dog both
the society and the company which succeeded it.

One of the legal tangles which faced the project was that
the old Light Railway Company—unlike the Talyllyn and
the Festiniog Railway Companies—had ceased to exist on
31 December 1922. If the British Transport Commission was
to assign its rights and obligations with regard to the W & L,
it had to be to a body approved by the Ministry of Transport.
Sounding out the Ministry for its views, it appeared that it
would be necessary to secure the incorporation of a limited
liability company to be responsible for operating the railway.
At first, some members expected that the society would continue with control over the company which it was now
proposed should be formed.

The spring of 1959 brought news of a provisional agreement and proposed terms which, hearteningly, seemed to be within the reach of the preservation organisation. With little hope of funds being forthcoming for the purchase of the railway, it was very fortunate that the somewhat unusual procedure of leasing the line was offered. The proposal was for a lease on a 42 year basis and the rolling stock was to be paid for by hire purchase over a ten year period—recalling the purchase of the first timber bolsters over half a century earlier. Agreement was subject to Ministry of Transport approval of the company carrying passengers. July 1959 saw the first working parties clearing the line, at first along the town section, and, as summer passed, on Golfa bank—where brambles were vieing with rapidly sprouting saplings for possession of the track. At about this time, a selection was made of the W & L rolling stock which was to be purchased. Apart from the two locomotives, for which considerable sums had to be raised in due course, a representative range of the freight stock was chosen.

The transfer of the latter from the Welshpool terminus to Raven Square or beyond seemed desirable, but the society had neither motive power nor legal powers to operate the railway. In September, while the agreement of BR to the movement of the stock awaited a report that clearance of the track had been completed to their satisfaction, a working party—in somewhat cavalier fashion—went ahead. They solved the haulage problem by borrowing a pair of sturdy carthorses which were newly shod for the occasion. Quite a number of trips were required to complete the movement, the steep gradients in some parts necessitating 'banking' at the rear provided by half a dozen society members.

THE COMPANY

The year 1960 brought with it an important event in the saga of the railway's preservation. On 4 January occurred the incorporation of the Welshpool and Llanfair Light Railway Preservation Company Ltd, to be followed five days later by the company's first meeting at a Paddington public house. Though well-advised, the formation of the company had not

(above) *Four of the last coaches to run on the Sierra Leone Railway were shipped to Liverpool and moved by road to Wales. They were transferred to W&L metals at Castle Caereinion station on 8 August 1975; (below) built in 1954 for the Sierra Leone Railway as No 85, this 2-6-2 tank locomotive arrived at the same time and has since performed very successfully*

Page 108 *LOCOMOTIVES – 1*

(above) The Countess *in lined works grey at the makers'*; (below) The Countess *in service near Cyfronydd circa*
1967

been achieved without a certain amount of controversy, and among those who resigned over the issue was the founder-secretary. The society lingered for over a year after the Company was incorporated. Finally, after a meeting in Birmingham on 11 March 1961, four and a half years after its formation, the society was wound up and its funds transferred to the new Company which most of the members had already joined.

Before incorporation, it had to be decided what kind of company was required. A private company would not have been appropriate but there are two main kinds of public company. One, like the original company which built the line, is open to all to subscribe to up to the limit of the share capital authorised. Here, the society would have had to acquire at least 51 per cent of the issued shares to retain control. Had such a company been set up, perhaps the offer of the remaining shares would have attracted not only some of the much-needed capital but also a greater flow of talented contributions towards the direction of the line. However, the principle of equal voting powers for all prevailed over all other considerations and the company formed was of the kind 'limited by guarantee and not having a share capital'.

One vote at the company's general meetings is gained by each person who pays the full membership subscription. This was felt to be a democratic formula appropriate to an organisation dependent upon the combined efforts of individual and manifold talents, freely donated in a crusading spirit. The inability of any individual to gain financial control of the company under this arrangement was particularly welcomed. Special provision was made for supporters under eighteen years old to pay a reduced subscription as non-voting associates.

The legal status of the newly registered company was a highly desirable feature in view of its engaging in trade of various kinds and the need for liability to the general public to devolve upon the company and not upon individual members. Disappointingly, many summer months were yet to wax and wane without public train services running, resulting in the loss of much-needed revenue and testing morale. However, spirits were boosted by the operation of special

trains for members. Many thrilled to the sound of the rever-
berating exhausts as the engines climbed Golfa bank. Throughout the year 1960, attempts were being made to work out
details of the lease. It was realised that, with the exclusion
of the Welshpool town section from the contract, the motive
power depot would have to be at Llanfair Caereinion. It
seemed that plans would have to be made for a new terminus
on the west of Raven Square. The unsuitability of this
arrangement resulted in a board representative visiting
Western Region headquarters where he was able to persuade
British Railways to amend the draft lease to include the line
as far east as the Standard Quarry. This would have given
much better scope for providing a new station with space
for congregating and the parking of cars. A term of 21 years
was, unfortunately, the longest that could now be wrung
out of the authorities at Paddington; neither was there
included any option to renew the lease on expiry.

Another winter passed before details of the proposed lease
were eventually agreed by both sides. By dint of judicious
negotiations, these terms had been kept within the scope
of the preservation company's rather precarious finances. A
relatively nominal initial rent had been agreed. For the first
five years, £100 was to be paid annually increasing thereafter
in two stages. The summer months of 1961 were occupied
with track clearing and the acquisition of the necessary
rolling stock. By November, it was possible to apply to the
Ministry of Transport for a Light Railway (Leasing and
Transfer) Order. It was four months later, in March 1962,
that the first visit took place from a Ministry official who
intimated what restrictions (with regard to speed and so on)
were likely to be imposed. Two months later came another
visit—this time mainly to discuss the position at Raven
Square. The official heard the company's views regarding the
siting of the terminus, but gave little hope of the Ministry
agreeing to the railway being allowed to run across the road
there on the level.

Some of the members were understandably becoming
weary of the continual postponement of the re-opening but,
at long last, on 3 October 1962 was issued the British Transport Commission (Welshpool and Llanfair) Light Railway

(Leasing and Transfer) Order. Effective from 12 October, it specified the south-west side of Raven Square as the eastern terminal. Of the loss of the crossing over Raven Square, the late Lt-Col Sir Thomas H. Salt BT., chairman of the company 1960-65, wrote:

'. . . the result of the line the Minister took will be felt through the years. In every way, the Railway will be harder to make a commercial success, less pleasant from the visitor's point of view and we will have to put up with second best solutions to countless problems not only at Raven Square but all over the Railway'.

TRAINS AGAIN

By the time the Order was eventually issued, a set of rolling stock had been acquired which was sufficient to satisfy the new management's basic requirements. Though acutely short of capital, the company overcame the complete lack of stock with pluck and initiative. By the autumn of 1962, the line possessed the original two locomotives—*The Earl* and *The Countess*, two 4-wheel diesel locomotives, two smaller motor trolleys and five modern bogie carriages. In addition, there was a collection of wagons and vans including stock suitable for permanent way work. Although one of the trolleys had been brought up from the old yard at Welshpool soon after working parties were allowed on the line, news of the first engine capable of hauling engineering trains was received with delight. It arrived on a Tuesday towards the end of March 1961—a modest enough, diesel powered machine. It was none the less welcomed and was named *Raven*, after the inn of that name at the Welshpool end of the line. Its departure from the Nettleton Top ironstone mines in Lincolnshire had unfortunately been postponed some months, partly through the delay in transit of a pair of new couplers which were to be fitted prior to dispatch. This diminutive machine was to perform heroically on the line.

Before the society was superseded by the new company, the search had begun for suitable coaching stock. This had led to an approach being made to the Admiralty and negotiations were eventually brought to a successful conclusion through the good offices of Sir Thomas, the w & l chairman. The Admiralty light railway from which the w & l acquired rolling stock for re-opening was one of the few 2ft 6in gauge lines built in Britain. It lay at Upnor on the north bank of the River Medway opposite Chatham dockyard in East Kent. The last scheduled service ran from Upnor to the terminus at Lodge Hill on 29 May 1961. Ill though it was for the Upnor line, this was the event which released the coaches so eagerly awaited at Welshpool.

Meanwhile, the w & l's two o–6–oT Beyer Peacock locomotives were in Oswestry Works. A price for them had been agreed with Western Region and early efforts to raise the sum required from members met with an encouraging response. Overhaul of the locomotives went ahead at Oswestry and in April 1961, *The Earl* was steamed for the first time for four and a half years. Friday, 28 July 1961 was one of the most exciting and significant days in the new company's history. On the previous day, *The Earl* had been dispatched for Welshpool on a br flat wagon. At the same time, a set of 2ft 6in gauge flat wagons and two semi-open coaches were being carried by rail from the Lodge Hill & Upnor Railway. A steam crane from Shrewsbury arrived at Welshpool on the morning of that Friday in July to find the new stock for the w & l waiting. The crane was propelled on to the Smithfield market siding. Alongside, a temporary extension of the 2ft 6in gauge had recently been laid as the permanent way in the narrow gauge yard had already been recovered. The lifting of the rolling stock on to w & l metals was watched with exultation as first *The Earl*, then the coaches and lastly the wagons were pushed down the siding. Crowds cheered from the lineside at the brave sight of a steam engine in action again as the stock was moved through the town to reach the loop sidings at Golfa and Castle Caereinion.

A members' open weekend held two months later was celebrated by the first steam workings from Welshpool to Llanfair since closure, five years previously. Members not only enjoyed the smooth riding of the newly acquired coaches but made good use of one of the new flat wagons marshalled in the train for photographers and tape recording enthusiasts. Later in the year, *The Earl* made several more trips through

Welshpool hauling quantities of ballast and sleepers transferred from BR wagons standing on the Smithfield siding. In
November, the Shrewsbury steam crane made a return visit
to Welshpool where seven more Upnor vehicles were ready
to be lifted off the standard gauge bogie wagons on to W & L
metals. Pride of this batch was the newer composite car.
Again, the operation was performed by using the Smithfield
market siding. Only three months later, the arrival became
imminent of yet another item of rolling stock—a 105bhp
Planet diesel locomotive. This, too, was from the Admiralty's
line in Kent, but this time the movement was by road. On
a cold, misty, February morning, *Upnor Castle* as it was to
become, was removed from the road lowloader by driving
it over temporary track on to the narrow gauge stub in
Welshpool yard.

The Countess was still in the workshops at Oswestry
undergoing heavy repairs and money was being sought to
meet the cost. Eventually, on an unusually sunny October
day in 1962—within a few days of her ladyship's sixtieth
birthday—*The Countess* returned home. Resplendent in her
new coat of paint, W & L locomotive No 2 travelled to Welshpool on a standard gauge wagon to be met by the Shrewsbury
steam crane which once again had turned out to effect the
transfer. After this was carefully and successfully accomplished, making use of the market siding, a start was made on
raising steam in *The Countess*. *The Earl* then came to 'meet
the wife', as a wag put it at the time, before setting off for
Llanfair hauling a special members' train. The engine was
decorated with a flag of the Welsh dragon and a string of
Union Jacks which, together with those hung out by the
people of Welshpool, lent to the occasion a suitably festive
air. After the special reached Llanfair, news came that *The
Countess* had left Welshpool although it was reported from
Golfa that the leading and trailing crank pin brasses were
running hot. However, she ran on to Castle Caereinion where
the returning special passed her. She ambled westwards, light,
to Llanfair—making the first trip to Llanfair for over six
years—while the special continued to Raven Square. Here
the train was gravity shunted past the locomotive and propelled through the town. Dusk was gathering as the return

journey began. Winding its way between the houses, *The Earl* left poised a path of languid smoke to complement the evening mist setting over the tumbled roofs of the town.

THE RE-OPENING

These were exciting days on the line. While the board was concerned about the mounting gap between available funds and the estimate of what was required, the Powis woods repeatedly resounded to the sounds of steam in action. Permanent way materials were collected from standard gauge wagons at Welshpool, and on at least one occasion double-heading was required—something never allowed in GWR days. Just before Christmas 1962 special passenger-carrying trains were put on for Llanfair fair—the first advertised public service since 1931. The winter that followed was a hard one during which *The Earl* was derailed at Cyfronydd crossing when the rails were packed with ice. However, inclement weather was unable to prevent volunteers from carrying out sufficient repairs to the track to satisfy the inspector from the Ministry of Transport when he visited the line on 26 March.

The great day for which everyone had worked for so long was Saturday, 6 April 1963—exactly sixty years after the first opening ceremony. As on the first occasion, the day dawned with threatening skies, but in contrast, and by way of a good omen, the weather later cleared and the sun appeared in time for the re-opening ceremony. Promptly at 11am, *The Earl* responded to the guard's whistle and set out manfully up the sharp incline from Welshpool narrow gauge yard, drawing two coaches conveying the chairman's party. The chairman, Sir Thomas Salt, accompanied by the Earl of Powis, alighted at Llanfair at about 12.10pm and mounted a flat wagon, the better to address the jostling crowd which had assembled in the yard. The Earl was due to go abroad and was having to change his arrangements slightly, little realising that sixty years before his predecessor had had to do something similar when he altered *his* plans and hurried back from overseas to preside at the official opening of the railway. The Earl contrasted his happy assignment with the gloomy news that had come that week of Dr Beeching's report recommending the drastic pruning of the national railway system. Wishing the W & L prosperity, the Earl walked to No 2 *The Countess* and drove the engine through the tape across the tracks before being presented with a memento of the occasion.

Following this ceremony, *The Countess* steamed out with the chairman's train bearing the guests to Welshpool where, repeating history, they repaired to the Royal Oak Hotel for luncheon. Meanwhile, a second party was refreshed in the Public Institute at Llanfair before being conveyed on a special train to Castle Caereinion and back. This train, which left Llanfair at 1.30pm, turned out to be the first public service of the new regime's first season. The return working of the chairman's special also carried fare-paying passengers, some of whom were allowed to ride free, at their own risk, from Welshpool to Castle. This last train on a great day arrived at Llanfair terminus at 4.00pm precisely.

Sadly, the year that saw passenger services restarted also saw the end of the Welshpool town section. Only two days

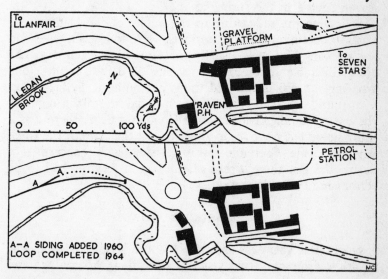

Raven Square. (*above*) 1903. Quarry siding later converted into loop, date unknown. (*below*) 1964 showing loop for projected Welshpool terminal

before the re-opening ceremony, Welshpool Borough Council completed the purchase of the railway from Raven Square eastwards, and soon afterwards the council decided that the company's trains would not be able to work over it after August of that year. On 17 August 1963 a genuine 'Last Train' ran through the town, spectacularly double-headed by *The Earl* and *The Countess*. Two days later, work on lifting the track commenced at the Church Street crossing. Few British railways have intermingled with road traffic or pushed past householders' back windows as this line had done in Welshpool. Now the final cut had finally come and not without causing bitterness on the part of some who believed it would bring more than just difficulties in transferring rail-borne materials. However, Welshpool's councillors were more concerned with the chance to extend the cattle market and car park and prepare for the construction of a 'bypass' along Brook Street. The final lengths of rail, near Raven Square, were lifted in November 1965. Meanwhile, a military detachment helping with engineering work on the line, had built a short loop and erected a stop-block on the west of Raven Square in the spring of 1964.

Following the re-opening to the public of the Llanfair and Castle Caereinion section, services were run each weekend and on bank holidays—usually three workings each day. The 1964 timetable involved two weeks of daily running (one working). It also introduced trains extending to Sylfaen after Whitsuntide of that year. The turn-round at Sylfaen required the use of the diesel locomotive *Upnor Castle* as there was a short siding but no loop. In August 1964 the state of the track beyond Castle Caereinion was causing such concern that during the last three weeks of the season services had to be terminated at Castle station.

A DISASTROUS BLOW

Before the year was out, much more serious trouble was to arise. After only two years of operating, the courage and hopes of the pioneer supporters were to receive a severe jolt. Wet weather prevailed in mid-Wales towards the end of 1964, a climatic characteristic for which the area tends to

be noted. As a result, the surging River Banwy at Llanfair
Caereinion rose higher and higher until an inspection party
found the menacing torrents flooding the track near Dolrhyd
Mill. Alas, this was not all. On Sunday morning, 13 December
1964, it was discovered to everyone's utmost dismay that the
viaduct carrying the railway over the river had sustained
serious damage during the night. The northern stone-built
pier had subsided and the girders dipped drunkenly above
the swirling current.

The sad news spread and it began to be realised what a
desperate position the company was in. The damaged bridge
prevented trains running further than Heniarth, just over a
mile and a quarter from Llanfair Caereinion. This could only
lead to lower passenger receipts and possibly the end of the
company in the form it had been established unless some
way of restoring the bridge could be found. But the company
had no capital reserves and considerable funds would be
required for a job of this size. The weeks following saw a
hectic series of discussions, Board meetings and consultations
with civil engineering advisors. Soon an idea of the cost of
rebuilding the bridge emerged—about £3,000 was estimated
as the probable figure. This news was circulated to members
together with details of the appeal fund which the chairman
had opened as soon as he heard of the disaster. Even if the
fund succeeded beyond the dreams of the most optimistic,
some way had to be found of getting the work done quickly
as well as cheaply. By a stroke of good fortune, it now
appeared that 'behind the scenes' the chairman was arranging
salvation in the form of a military exercise.

Although the appeal fund was still well short of the target,
the response was so promising that the Board felt able to give
the 'go ahead' when the 16th Railway Regiment Royal
Engineers finally agreed to do the work, having worked out
realistic costings and a plan of action. Volunteers now set
to work to remove the decking, track and timbers from the
sagging girders. In April, a detachment of Royal Engineers
arrived and set up camp alongside the bridge. Light steel
trestling was brought and lowered on to the river bed by
crane on the Llanfair side and by rope from the locomotive
Upnor Castle on the other side. Trestle frames were properly

positioned and then the task of lifting the girders began by using jacks. This allowed the demolition of the drunken pier with the aid of pneumatic drills.

Work started next on a coffer dam intended to provide a dry area in which to build a new pier. Flooding and strong currents caused great difficulties and the Royal Engineers had to leave before the dam was completed. However, they returned at the end of July by which time the dam was finished and most of the remains of the old pier removed, despite continuing difficulties with water leaking through the coffer dam. By dint of various expedients it was possible to drill the river bed and fix anchoring pins on which a new steel pier was to be erected. Lorries brought concrete to the bank on the Heniarth side and this was ferried in wheelbarrows over planks to secure the foundations. When the erection of the pier was completed, the girders were lowered on to it and the trestles removed. The soldiers followed this by expeditiously replacing the decking and track, and relaying the track from the bridge to Heniarth station where the loop was re-laid as two sidings. At 11.0am on Friday, 13 August, eight months after the floods, *Upnor Castle* crossed the bridge safely. On the following afternoon the first pas-

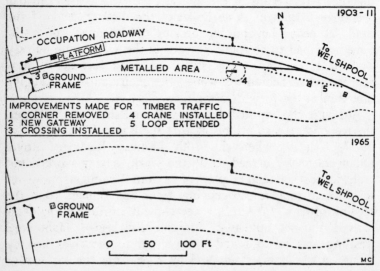

Heniarth

senger train edged its way across as services to Castle
Caereinion were resumed, subject to speed restrictions in
the area of the bridge.

By a strange irony another disaster touched the railway
on the very next day, although of a personal nature. This
was the death of the chairman, Sir Thomas Salt, 'who had
led the company through many adversities, not least the
bridge calamity. Sir Thomas, who had had connections with
the old North Staffordshire Railway, had been chairman of
the preservation company since its formation. Many members
recall the way he inspired them in the days before public
services started. Sometimes, when travelling the line on a
members' 'special', Sir Thomas was known to have stood up
on one of the flat wagons to address the members present,
outlining the problems to be faced and spurring them on to
continued effort. In his last days, Sir Thomas had the satisfaction of knowing that what had seemed like an insuperable
problem with regard to the river viaduct had been overcome.

KEEPING GOING

While engineering works on the line were in progress in
1965, passenger trains ran only to Heniarth. When services
were restored in August, two trains were run each day (three
at weekends), though once again they terminated at Castle
Caereinion. The pattern now established for the ensuing
years was a daily service with two or three trains in the
high summer (July to mid-September), and services at weekends and bank holidays for the rest of the season. Since 1967
five trains each day have been required on the busiest days
of the bank holidays. Indeed, in 1968, after the arrival of
further coaching stock from Austria, even five trains were
insufficient at peak times and duplicate trains had to be run.
Special trains for party bookings run at various times during
the season, diesel-hauled on rare occasions. Sometimes they
are photographic trips, with the chance of open accommodation on a flat wagon and with extra stops for photography
at picturesque spots.

Although public services became so well established and
although even the desperate problem of the Banwy bridge

was miraculously solved, the railway continued to be plagued by grave difficulties, mainly financial. In fact, the preservation company had been desperately short of capital right from the start. Even before the flood damage of December 1964 at least five special appeals for money for the proper operation of the railway went out to members, in addition to such appeals as that for saving *The Countess*. In 1961, £5,000 was being sought, and when only a fraction of this materialised winding-up was threatened. Nevertheless, with the overdraft soaring and the decision taken to abandon running to Welshpool, services had opened and, promisingly, membership increased. In the year the river bridge collapsed, another appeal for funds had already been put out along with another threat of winding-up. The bridge appeal, when it came, had been on a public basis; this helps to explain the amazing response which produced sufficient money for restoration to go ahead. Meanwhile, membership subscriptions had to be raised to help reduce the overdraft. The closure of the bridge during rebuilding in the spring and summer of 1965 unfortunately delayed the hoped-for build-up of traffic revenue.

In the closing years of the 1960s progress was slower than many would have liked and even essential maintenance on track and locomotives was acutely hampered by lack of funds. If there was impatience at the non-availability of materials, it was not always widely realised that at the end of most seasons the company found itself with a continuing overdraft. Often, little cash was left over after running the services to buy supplies, although sometimes generous gifts in cash or kind prevented renovation from coming to a standstill. Despite these difficulties the rehabilitation proceeded of track which had deteriorated over many years. Each winter, with the cessation of passenger services, a new section was completely relaid with sound sleepers and fresh ballast. As each year passed the sections relaid became longer, and in the autumn of 1968 it became possible to replace the earlier pick and shovel methods with a bulldozer for clearing the trackbed. The winter of 1969–70 saw further mechanisation. Not only was a bulldozer hired, but afterwards lorries lurched along the trackbed to deliver the ballast without transhipment. A mechanical drill was used to prepare the

sleepers for the spikes and electric tamping hammers helped
with packing and consolidating the ballast. It was a boost to
the morale of weekend permanent way workers.

Alterations to the track layout were also made as the demand
and opportunity arose. A year after re-opening the lifted
siding at Sylfaen was put back, while in 1967 a new siding
was laid at Cyfronydd to accommodate wagon stock. The
loop at Castle station had already been extended in the
spring of 1966 to permit the turn-round of longer trains.

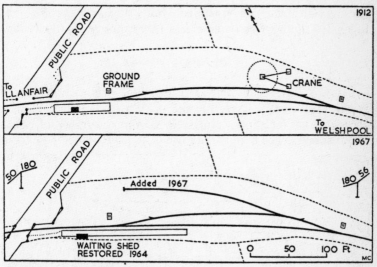

Cyfronydd. The shed was once a LNWR van. Siding lifted 1980.

During the years which succeeded the re-opening ceremony, the question of running from Castle Caereinion to
Welshpool continued to be raised. As the months passed,
there was sobering realisation that membership numbers were
not increasing significantly and that all funds were being
swallowed for operating the Llanfair—Castle section. As
experience was accumulated, prospects of an early extension
of services to Welshpool receded. Nevertheless, tentative
plans were made. In the spring of 1966 a scheme was
announced to run to Sylfaen the next year and to extend
special workings to Welshpool in 1969. Soon after the
announcement, locomotive No 5 *Nutty* reached Raven Square

on two occasions including a trip with weed-killing apparatus. But the year 1969 arrived without it having been possible to renovate the track between Castle Caereinion and Welshpool. In addition, there were difficulties (mainly financial) in providing the automatic braking on coaching stock which the MOT inspector required for working public services on the dramatically graded Golfa bank. The short run-round loop and lack of station facilities at Raven Square were further handicaps. One proposal to overcome these problems envisaged a diesel-hauled shuttle service with one, or two, coaches connecting with the steam-hauled trains at Castle or Sylfaen. Ingenious though this scheme was, it was not really a solution.

LLANFAIR STATION

Llanfair Caereinion terminus was not originally regarded as the ideal headquarters for the project. It is not as readily accessible as Welshpool and suffers from a number of other disadvantages. The cramped nature of the site hampered efforts

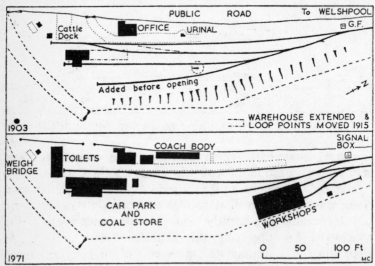

Llanfair Caereinion station

to make it attractive to the visiting public. Car parking space was severely limited, especially as the premises were shared with a group of coal merchants until 1972. The area had to accommodate the company's workshops, while the corrugated iron warehouse dating from the opening (nowadays used for engineering stores) was sited awkwardly for visitors entering the station.

The south (coal road) siding was inconveniently situated and was therefore removed. A headshunt was then installed on the east and a locomotive inspection pit afterwards added. During 1967 the existing brick-built signal box was brought into use—not without having roused controversy among members regarding the necessity of signalling. The eight-lever frame now in use was salvaged from the main-line signal box at Llanbrynmair. In the south-east corner of the station was a steeply banked area, previously unused—except for vegetable growing in World War I. This was eventually chosen as the site for a two-road locomotive shed and carriage workshop. Excavations began in 1967, and over the next four years the building gradually took shape, largely constructed by volunteers. The steelwork was secondhand and was only erected with the aid of considerable ingenuity. It was possible to bring the north road into use on 14 June 1970 and install the second road during the following year.

The old standard gauge coach bodies installed for storage by the GWR were converted by the present administration for volunteers' sleeping quarters. Eventually the company was able to provide superior accommodation and the surviving coachbodies were dismantled in September 1969 to make way for a former Eastern Region 1st class sleeping car No E1260E. Passengers welcomed the introduction of a mobile tea-bar which arrived in time for the 1967 season. Further facilities for passengers were provided in March 1970, when a brick-built toilet block was erected—this time by contractors. Subsequently, the teabar and sleeping car were replaced.

NEW ARRIVALS

Events rousing particular excitement have been the arrival of further useful pieces of rolling stock as they became available. On 8 May 1966, the unconventional locomotive, *Monarch*, arrived by road and the diminutive *Nutty* struggled to haul the $28\frac{1}{2}$ ton articulated Bagnall on to W & L metals.

Early in 1968, the o–6–o Drewry diesel locomotive was secured, and the low-loader road vehicle which transported *Chattenden* from Cumberland left Llanfair conveying *Upnor Castle* for the Festiniog Railway—and regauging. A momentous occasion soon afterwards was the coming of the Austrian coaching stock. Mutual interest and exchange visits of officials had been established for some time with the busy narrow gauge Zillertal Railway in the Tyrol. It is intriguing that the Zillertalbahn and other Austrian lines were built to the 760mm gauge and not 750mm which seems more logical—but it has been fortunate for the W & L. Early in 1964 the transfer of some surplus passenger vehicles from the Zillertalbahn to the W & L was first mooted, but for four years financial and other considerations held up progress. However, as traffic mounted in Wales, the demand for more passenger accommodation became pressing at peak times. At last, the good news was received that on 25 March 1968 the transfer had started of four end-balcony saloon coaches. They were transported over the systems of the Austrian, German and Belgian railways to Ostend. Belgian Marine vessels ferried them to Dover where British Rail took over on 9 April. Two days later, a special train of four well-flats brought the Continental saloons into Welshpool station where members had been awaiting their arrival throughout the day.

Although the dusk of evening was already gathering, two of the coaches, Nos 24 and 16, were craned in turn on to a road vehicle and moved through the town to the level crossing at New Drive. This point, at the foot of Golfa bank, was easily accessible from the main road. A mobile crane gingerly lifted the new stock on to Welsh metals and the Drewry diesel locomotive drew them cautiously up to Golfa loop for the night. There was elation that the operation was going so well and that the coaches appeared to run on the Welsh track better than anyone had dared to hope. Soon after first light the next day—a beautifully sunny morning—work began on moving the remaining two coaches in similar fashion. The diesel locomotive *Chattenden* inched the vehicles up to Golfa station where the whole rake was coupled up. For some months previously, members had been clearing overhanging vegetation in anticipation of the delivery of the 8ft wide

Page 125 *LOCOMOTIVES – 2*

(above) *0-4-4-0T* Monarch *soon after arrival at Llanfair and before fitting of the new chimney;* (below) *a sleeping giant from Finland. Built by the Belgian Tubize concern for the Jokioisten Railway, this impressive locomotive was put on display in 1983*

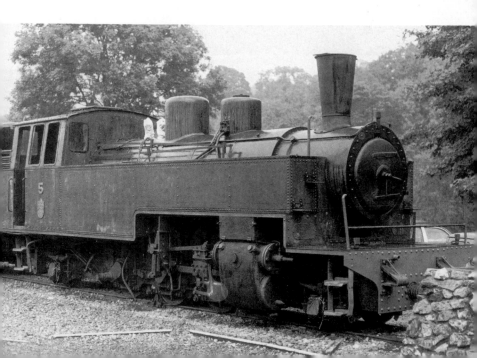

(above left) *Makers' photograph of four-ton open wagon;* (left) *flat wagon with removable sides for livestock;* (below) *private-owned four-ton wagon registered no 601/1903*

saloons on to the unused section. Extreme caution was never-theless observed as the train continued towards Llanfair Caereinion.

The arrival coincided with the start of the Easter holiday and the novelty of the new rolling stock helped to attract record numbers of Easter visitors. Many were carried in the Zillertalbahn saloons which, after hasty cleaning, had to be rushed into use on the day immediately after they reached Llanfair. Holiday times during the year continued to bring overwhelming crowds of visitors.

With the line's popularity growing, a search began for more motive power. It was realised that without reserve funds for major repairs to Nos 1 and 2, and with the demise of the steam locomotive accelerating everywhere, it would be wise policy to obtain useful specimens in sound condition as the oppor-tunity arose. As a result, another link was struck with Austria. This time, a visit was paid to the 760mm Steiermarkische Landesbahnen which threaded the picturesque Alpine valleys between Ratten and Weiz, about 20km from the valley resort of Graz.

At Weiz, an interesting o–8–oT locomotive was for disposal which had been built for the German military authorities in World War II. Inspection confirmed that it was in very good shape overall and there was reason to believe that the all-important boiler condition was most promising. Arrange-ments went ahead swiftly and just after 6.oopm on Thursday, 11 December 1969, the locomotive was hauled on to the line in Llanfair Caereinion station yard. The mid-winter darkness had already descended and members' car headlights were pressed into service to illuminate the scene. Movement had started from Weiz eight days previously. A low-loading road trailer was used and, after traversing Germany and Holland, it travelled by ferry from Amsterdam to Immingham in Lincolnshire.

Plans to build up the motive power stock hardly envisaged movements half way across the world. However, a visitor to the island of Antigua in the West Indies spotted the o–6–2 tank locomotive *Joan* disused and rusting at the government sugar factory. Its specifications well suited it for work on the w & L. Purchasing was easy but then a number of daunting hurdles had

to be overcome. These included the finding of a shipping company able to handle the load, movement to the wharf despite
the branch line to the port being abandoned, a political furore on
the island about the sale to 'imperialists'—and the appearance
of a rival bidder from the USA. Incredibly, the news came that
Joan had been loaded on to the *Booker Valiance* on 20 October
1971, during the cool of the night. The ship sailed for a tour of
Caribbean and South American ports and then crossed to Liverpool. At last, the Kerr Stuart was home!

EVENTFUL YEARS

Welsh narrow gauge railways tend to provide idyllic scenery
for passengers to enjoy at the 'country' terminus. Castle
Caereinion was no exception. After the journey from Llanfair,
first threading the river banks and later rising up unbelievably
steep grades, travellers were treated to the panorama of hill
masses stretching towards Snowdon while the engine crew
prepared to return. But the track curved further uphill between
high banks, beckoning eastwards. Unfortunately, a great deal
of work was required to make the next section fit for passenger
trains again.

In summer 1970 with the financial position improving, plans
were announced for rebuilding the line between Castle and
Sylfaen. Volunteers toiled throughout that summer season lifting
the disintegrating sleepers, digging out and clearing the trackbed and laying in sound sleepers. Within earshot of trains and
tourists arriving and departing from Castle station below,
members continued to drill and hammer and shovel as rails
were spiked down and packed and ballasted. Scout groups and
parties from schools lent a hand.

The following year the assault was transferred nearer to
Sylfaen. Where the line parallels the Sylfaen Brook, foxgloves,
brambles and bushes had taken over and trees spanned the
railway. As clearing progressed, an engineering train pushed
through to Pussy Bridge where the watercourse passes obliquely
below the line. Here, reconstruction with a new concrete invert
was essential. Another season of track building followed. The
remaining section, the steep bank east of Coppice Lane crossing
was tackled the next year by a dedicated group of members

who devoted an early season holiday to an all out period of
railway 'navvying'.

Finally, on 15 July 1972, Castle station was decked out with
flags and bunting in readiness for a suitably elaborate re-opening
ceremony. No 10 *Sir Drefaldwyn*, appropriately decorated and
piloting No 1 *The Earl*, simmered while speeches were delivered.
Then with the Mayor of Welshpool at the controls, the train
broke a ceremonial tape and climbed towards Sylfaen.

At the new terminus, the wilderness of mud, nettles and
brambles had given way to a new gravel platform 170ft long,
constructed on the main line to the west of the siding reinstated
in 1964. Space had never been provided for a loop line. The
train engine therefore ran into a newly overhauled spur while a
second locomotive—usually a diesel—drew the train past the
points. After the train engine had backed on, the return to
Llanfair could begin. A year after the re-opening, reconstruction of the main road alongside the station gave vastly improved
access albeit sacrificing the hedgerows and attractive grassy
banks.

Of course Welshpool remained the ultimate goal. When the
tenth anniversary of the line's re-opening approached, the idea
was born of special members' trains to Raven Square. These
could be seen as a token of intent—if something could be done
about the jungle-like wilderness that had sprung up between
Golfa and Raven Square. A contractor with agricultural equipment was engaged to cut a way through, tunnel-like. Seeing a
pipe dream evolving into reality, work parties turned out to
undertake makeshift repairs to the track while arrangements
were made for water to be supplied by the Montgomery Water
Board from their hydrant at New Drive crossing.

The Earl with three coaches reached Welshpool at 12.25 on
12 May 1973. The successful descent of the long and notorious
Golfa incline was marked by exultant and sustained whistling
from the veteran locomotive and as it arrived at Raven Square,
it was watched by a great gallery of spectators massed along
the main road. The Mayor of Welshpool and others welcomed
the train. *The Earl* worked another special during the afternoon
no less successfully. On the following day however, wet conditions for the third run taxed the crew's skill as the gallant
machine slipped to a halt on the treacherously steep banks.

Truly a memorable weekend, it inspired members, attracted publicity and underlined the Company's determination to re-open public services to Welshpool.

It is perhaps inevitable that any enterprise will meet with minor crises. But with initiative, hard work and lucky breaks, the w & l has coped. Early on Monday 6 August 1973, the most disastrous floods for several years struck mid-Wales. Storms brought 4in of rain in 24 hours; the Banwy and the Vyrnwy burst their banks. At dawn, water was racing over the part of the line from the old water tower to Schoolmistress's Cottage near Heniarth and at the Banwy Bridge the torrent rose to within two feet of the cross girders. Luckily, fears for the safety of the bridge were not realised though a huge tree trunk was found wedged against the steel pier as the water receded. Near Dolrhyd Mill, ballast had been carried away and discarded sleepers tossed about but no serious damage had been done. Services were suspended but they resumed on the following day.

Details have been given on page 110 of how the taking over of the line from br was made possible by negotiating a lease on quite advantageous terms. Nevertheless, the outright purchase of the railway was a most desirable objective. It would safeguard the future beyond 1983 and provide more favourable conditions for major investment. The news that br had offered to sell the line including all land and buildings came as a welcome 10th anniversary present. Negotiations on terms moved slowly but favourably and on 12 March 1974 the Preservation Company became the owners of the railway. To meet the cost of £8000, an appeal had been launched. A substantial contribution was made by the then Welshpool Borough Council while the Wales Tourist Board helped with a loan repayable over 15 years. At last, the preservationists seemed to be getting tangible support from outside the membership.

Another successful initiative was the Railway Letter Service. In earlier times, the original w & l and the Cambrian Railways Co had tried in vain to gain permission to carry mails. The Preservation Co gained approval on its first application and the service began on 13 August 1975. The specially designed stamps and first day covers have since become much sought after – and provide a useful source of revenue.

MAINTENANCE AND IMPROVEMENTS

It is little less than astonishing that services on the W & L have been reliably maintained by all-volunteer crews, and that the timetable has been expanded. Not only does this involve the training of personnel who in their normal everyday life might be anything from an accountant to a welder, or a company secretary to a lorry driver's mate, but it is also necessary to arrange for a nucleus of such members to attend on the large number of days that the services operate. Many people were originally sceptical about the viability of such a scheme, but it has worked quite well. Continuity of control has been achieved since 1962 by the engagement of a general manager on a full-time basis, a post first filled by Mr M. M. Polglaze and later by Mr R. T. Russell.

Specialists—all volunteers—take charge of the various departments such as those responsible for the permanent way, locomotives, carriages and wagons and sales. Members who do not visit the line very frequently welcome a magazine produced quarterly which includes progress reports. Maintenance work and a rehabilitation programme have continued throughout each year largely dependent on volunteer support. The winter months have been earmarked for major trackwork to avoid interrupting summer services. For many years, starting in 1974 a week in October was designated for the complete rebuilding of a section of line, frequently as much as quarter of a mile. Such flurries of activity were possible as a result of a substantial team of members arranging to spend an autumn holiday together on the railway.

A particularly notable programme was embarked upon in October 1976, following the acquisition of a piece of somewhat low-lying land at Sylfaen and the granting of planning permission for alterations. All the track through the station was lifted together with 400yd on the western approach, ready for levelling by excavator. A procession of lorries brought new ballast and large quantities of stone rubble to widen the trackbed on the north side of what had been the platform. Work began on realigning the main line over the widened formation, the site for a new platform and on laying a 120yd loop line on the south side. Within three weeks, the station was reopened for a charter train.

As much of the traffic depended on visitors who arrived by car, adequate parking space was important. At Llanfair station, an improvement was achieved for the 1974 season by re-aligning the trackwork. The platform line and loop were relaid slightly nearer the main road after part of the station perimeter had been excavated to provide platform space. The siding was replaced by a shorter spur on a more northerly alignment.

Nearly three years later a strip of field was acquired for an extension of the headshunt to make more provision for storing rolling stock. Limited facilities at Llanfair had long meant that sidings at Heniarth and Cyfronydd had to be utilised for the storage of wagon stock and coaches. Later, the opportunity occurred to purchase an area of uneven, unused ground opposite the site of the old Tanllan timber dock, east of the station limits. Considerable earthmoving produced a suitable formation and the first of three carriage sidings was completed in August 1975. Beyond this point, the main line passed the picturesque old water tower by the river. Unfortunately, the supply from a nearby stream was becoming increasingly unreliable and in 1979 a new water tower was erected on brick piers in Llanfair station.

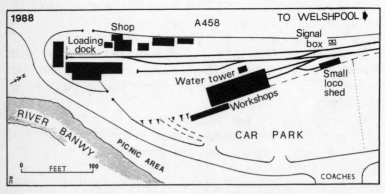

Llanfair station after improvements

At a time when there was a good deal of encouragement for schemes to relieve mounting unemployment, Montgomery District Council decided to purchase the meadows between Llanfair

station and the River Banwy. The Council planned to construct
an approach road, several advance factories and a site for the
W & L to take (on a 10 year mortgage) and develop as coach
and car parks. The old entrance to Llanfair station disappeared.
By Easter 1980, there was a decidedly superior access to the
south side of the station and the new car park.

AMBITIONS ABROAD AND AT HOME

It had long been hoped to run with vacuum braked stock. The
sharp changes of gradient on the western section of the line
made this highly desirable while such provision was a prerequisite of operating public services to Welshpool. As most of
the Upnor coaches were unsuited for fitting automatic brakes,
sources of fully fitted stock were being investigated in 1974,
mainly in the Isle of Man and Yugoslavia. Further afield, the
Sierra Leone Railway was closing down and though the idea of
extending the search to West Africa seemed ambitious, W & L
representatives were sent out to Freetown. Shortly afterwards,
negotiations were opened with the demolition contractor.

On 7 August 1975, a complete train was landed at Liverpool.
It was a red letter day for the W & L: four modern high
capacity coaches and a handsome prairie tank engine had been
brought across the Atlantic despite competition from a West
German scrap dealer, tenuous communications and a dock
strike in West Africa. The 2–6–2 Hunslet tank locomotive
reached Llanfair by road the same day while the remarkable
procession of vehicles conveying the coaches halted near
Sylfaen, continuing next day to Castle station. Here two mobile
cranes accomplished the unloading in brilliant sunshine. In all,
the operation cost over £14,000 met from an appeal fund, a
much appreciated grant from the Wales Tourist Board and an
interest-free loan from two members.

The 75th anniversary year of the railway was marked by the
organisation of special events on the weekend of 13/14 May
1978. On each day, seven passenger services were operated
using *Joan*, *Sir Drefaldwyn*, *Monarch* and the ex-Sierra Leone
Railway locomotive in turn. Trains were crossed at Castle
Caereinion. *The Earl* worked a freight train of original stock
for photographic purposes and the former gasworks locomotive

Dougal steamed along the line with some of the Upnor goods stock. Never before had so many engines been in steam at once on the line. The Talyllyn Railway co-operated by arranging special events at Tywyn; joint rover tickets, joint publicity and a novel connecting bus service contributed to the success of the weekend.

The surprising idea of the w & l taking on ten employees suddenly developed when the government-sponsored Manpower Services Commission offered a grant in 1976 to cover the wages for an initial period of six months. The w & l's project was accepted as part of the Job Creation Scheme which aimed to provide employment for young people. The project entailed one gang replacing fences west of Sylfaen and another gang clearing the scrub and trees on the Welshpool section. Though the work was important, it was difficult to accomplish with voluntary labour. The new grant-funded schemes were seen as a golden opportunity and when the first project ended, it was to be followed by a series of others including some devoted to specified work on rolling stock.

Hopes of running services to Welshpool never died and inspired sporadic efforts to improve the disused section although doubts were cast on the future of the existing terminus at Raven Square with news of plans for trunk road improvement in the area. One troublespot lay at Dead Man's Tree, half a mile down the incline below Golfa station. The track was shored up on timbers probably installed in post-war years after the formation had subsided following a culvert collapse. In summer 1974, new concrete culvert sections were obtained ready for rebuilding. Then, near New Drive crossing, lower down, the unwelcome discovery was made of a new washout. With collapse imminent, the track was promptly shored up until the embankment and the drainage could be rebuilt. The following year, the job of reconstructing the formation at Dead Man's Tree was successfully completed.

The impetus was growing as was pressure from various quarters for properly devised and co-ordinated plans to reopen to Welshpool especially with the advent of vacuum braked stock. In August 1976, the board of the Company announced that a scheme had been adopted and costed; steps were being taken to apply for financial assistance and the submission was being made for the planning permission required for a new station at Raven Square. Welshpool Town Council was reported to be enthusiastic.

In May 1977, the plan was launched at a public meeting in Birmingham with the publication of a prospectus and an appeal for £63,000. The project involved rebuilding the whole line from Sylfaen to Welshpool, a distance of 2.62 miles (4.2km). This was to entail clearing the trees and bushes from fence to fence, lifting the old track, re-laying on new stone ballast with new sleepers and constructing a terminus of spacious dimensions. The purchase of another, more powerful, diesel locomotive was envisaged for emergency use.

In due course land was leased alongside the old line near Raven Square and a safe access was eventually negotiated from the main road. It was intended to build a terminal layout with ample siding and platform space, full station facilities and a large car park. In all, this was to be the most costly and ambitious project the Preservation Co had entertained; ultimately, costs were to rise well beyond the original estimate. However, the time was ripe for this initiative. Help was at hand in the shape of grants from the Manpower Services Commission for labour to carry out much of the clearance and trackwork. Meanwhile, representations brought the W & L the pleasurable embarrassment of simultaneous offers of funds from the Wales Tourist Board and the Development Board for Rural Wales. The latter body's offer of £20,000 was accepted while the struggle to find the balance involved raising donations, an interest-free loan scheme, sponsored walks and even the sale of the four Upnor coaches without vacuum brakes. An exhibition explaining the project and mounted in one of the Sierra Leone coaches at Llanfair station proved popular and raised more funds.

An ingenious idea was the attempt to import steel sleepers from the dismantled 2ft 6in gauge Sierra Leone Railway. It was resolved to rebuild the line to high standards thus vastly reducing the need for expensive maintenance and replacement in the future. Unfortunately, political disputes and lack of co-operation in Sierra Leone defeated the W & L. With the project delayed, it was decided to buy 5000 new hardwood sleepers from Australia.

At Raven Square, a great deal of work was needed to transform swampy meadows into the Welshpool terminal. Contractors with machinery helped. A new channel about 150yd long was excavated into which the Sylfaen Brook was diverted along the southern edge of the site. The original track descended on a grade of 1 in 58 along the other side but the new station had to be on the level. Vast quantities of material were tipped and after several months the old stream meanders had been filled in and the formation had risen, partly on embankment.

Meanwhile, a project supervisor was engaged charged with organising the extension works and overseeing the labour provided under the Manpower Services Commission schemes. Removal of the old track began at Golfa prior to work on the drainage and the excavation of cuttings to ease the tightest curves. Lorries arriving with the new ballast were directed along the trackbed. Meanwhile, a base was established at Castle station for drilling the new sleepers and as they were hauled to the railhead on Golfa incline, re-laying proceeded rapidly. The sections below New Drive crossing and west of Golfa were similarly dealt with in turn.

The year 1981 brought an all-out effort by volunteers. New rail on brand new formation linked the old route with the new station layout. Here, pointwork, tracklaying, the provision of passenger access and water had all to be undertaken. Meanwhile, MSC trainees were re-laying Sylfaen bank. It was a race against time.

Nevertheless, on 4 July, 'Sir Drefaldwyn' – on crew training – became the first steam locomotive to reach the new station. Shortly afterwards, after a final inspection, the Department of Transport sanctioned the re-opening of the Welshpool section – on a 'one engine in steam' basis for the time being.

The great day so many had awaited for so long was 18 July 1981. 'Sir Drefaldwyn' entered Raven Square station about midday, the triumphant and prolonged whistling echoing in welcome from the tree clad slopes tilting skywards all round. Jubilant crowds were addressed by Welshpool's Mayor and the Company Chairman before the train left, its single Sierra Leone coach filled with contributors to the Appeal Fund. At 3.05pm, the first public train from Welshpool to Llanfair was packed and necessitated double heading. With no buildings, van 213 served as a ticket office. The short, temporary, sleeper-edged platform and the wagon-mounted 800 gallon tank for water supplies were all signs of the improvisation which had ensured the target date was met.

Financial constraints prevented the full implementation of the plan for the Welshpool terminus but work went ahead to construct a substantial platform, and a permanent water tower. A former L & NWR tappet locking frame from Groeslon near Caernarvon was installed in a signalbox ingeniously designed to incorporate a ticket office and this was in use when the official re-opening ceremony was performed by the Earl of Powis on 16 May 1982.

Over fifty years after the GWR had closed passenger services, trains ran regularly again between Welshpool and Llanfair. The Golfa incline proved a fearsome challenge to footplate crews and aficionados revelled in the sound of vintage locomotives blasting up the climb of 300ft in only a mile.

Yet passenger numbers did not expand as hoped. Special events were organised to remedy this including an augmented service for a Festival of Transport which became an annual event attended by numerous vintage road vehicles. Some of these occasions saw every serviceable coach in use and four locomotives. Once staff and ticket working was extended to Welshpool, in 1984, using a black, hexagonal staff, trains could pass at Sylfaen where a blockman was stationed. For four years, trains crossed here as a regular feature of the high season timetable but in 1988, the normal service reverted to operation with one train only. However, the period of operation was extended to match changing tourist trends.

Now passenger numbers were showing improvement and membership was at record levels. The return to service of No 2 'The Countess' was a landmark and another was the line's first ever Santa trains at Christmas 1987—both profitable and jolly. Crowds of wide eyed children travelled along the Banwy valley to collect Santa from his grotto. Meanwhile, at Llanfair, a workshop extension went ahead while plans were made and money raised for a long awaited carriage shed. Moves were afoot, too, to secure the help of local authorities and other agencies in the provision of a substantial building at Raven Square station.

A quarter of a century after the W & L re-opened, the endeavours of many dedicated volunteers had achieved a

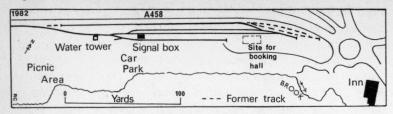

Welshpool (Raven Square) station

remarkable transformation. While the intermediate halts retain much of the rustic simplicity they exhibited in 1903, the wide approaches and spacious car parking areas at both termini underline the changed role of the railway. Indeed, the boost which it gives to the tourist trade of mid-Wales is increasingly appreciated. Traffic figures may be considerably higher for narrow gauge railways in more traditional holiday areas but on the W & L the scale of operations has allowed the preservationists to succeed in working the railway almost entirely by voluntary efforts.

Bequeathed to us is no ordinary branch line. The W & L surely represents one of the best examples of a rural line built under the auspices of the 1896 Light Railways Act, serving a community rather than a special traffic and built unsophisticatedly as was implicit in the Act. Use of the narrow gauge, tangling with the town and piercing the hill country with grinding curves and capricious gradients, truly tapped the Act's same spirit of purpose. This turn-of-the-century solution to the problem is of considerable interest in an era when public transport in thinly peopled rural areas is on the verge of annihilation. The preservation enterprise is safe-guarding for posterity a rare instance (in Britain) of the 2ft 6in gauge, chosen for its flexibility and economy with minimum sacrifice of capacity for handling substantial loads. Under a new, truly amateur regime, the future seems promising. May the shrill shriek of a steam locomotive whistle long echo and re-echo across the hills of Powys.

CHAPTER SEVEN

Locomotives and Rolling Stock—1901-1956

THE CONTRACTOR'S STOCK

For the construction contract Messrs Strachan used at least three narrow gauge locomotives and one of standard gauge for shunting in Welshpool yard. Of the 2ft 6in gauge locomotives the best documented is *Strachan No 9*, which left W. G. Bagnall's Castle Engine Works, Stafford, on 17 September 1901 for delivery new to the w & l contract. This was a standard locomotive of the makers' Margaret class, being an 0-4-0 saddle tank with inside frames, outside cylinders 7in by 12in and 1ft 9½in diameter wheels at 3ft 6in wheelbase. The characteristic Bagnall circular firebox was fitted, destined to reappear on the line in vastly larger guise over sixty years later. The makers' number was 1655.

A further locomotive which can be identified on this contract was built by the Hunslet Engine Company, Leeds, in 1883, makers' number 307. This was a standard type 0-4-0 saddle tank to 2ft 6in gauge with 7in by 10in cylinders and 1ft 8in wheels, delivered new to the Twywell Iron Ore Company Limited, Northants. It was employed at the Woodford Mines, Twywell, until transferred about 1890 to the Gretton Pits of E. P. Davis. This latter site in the Corby area was closed about 1900 and the locomotive disposed of. By chance the existence of the little Hunslet at Welshpool was revealed by an enquiry to Bagnall from Strachan for spares in autumn 1902, unfortunately without mention of the contractor's running number.

The identity of the third narrow gauge engine known to have been on the contract is much more obscure. The photograph of the Banwy Bridge, reputedly taken in 1902, shows a tiny engine standing on the centre span which is certainly not a standard type of the well known builders. It was a cabless 0–4–0 side or pannier tank with outside frames and cylinders. The tanks extend to the front of the smokebox and just discernible on them is the legend *Strachan No 8*. The only clue as to the builder lies in the large oval plate on the cabside, the style of which closely resembles that carried by products of the Falcon Engine Works, Loughborough, in the late 1880s, or just possibly those of Black, Hawthorn and Company Limited of Gateshead at about the same period.

The 4ft 8½in gauge locomotive used on the contract was built by Hunslet, makers' number 365, and supplied new in September 1885 to the contractors Holme and King at Brentwood, Essex. This was *Phyllis*, an 0–4–0 saddle tank with 10in by 15in cylinders and 2ft 9in wheels. Strachan was using this engine at a contract at Stafford in 1897 and later transferred it to Welshpool. Photographs exist which show this locomotive, named *Strachan No 3*, at Welshpool and also on his Tanat Valley contract 1899–1904. Of the contractors rolling stock there is little record. Bagnall supplied new steel V type tipping wagons in 1902 and old prints show wooden bodied tippers.

There was an auction of Strachan's equipment at Standard Quarry, Welshpool, on 15 May 1903. It is strange that such an event aroused little interest on the part of local press and we are left to ponder on the fate of much of the stock. Of the locomotives, Bagnall 1655 was definitely not sold. The makers supplied spares for it in June 1903, suggesting that some contractors' work was still proceeding—indeed the Bagnall tipping wagons were still in use in August 1903. By September 1903, however, Bagnall 1655 had been transferred to Strachan's contract for the construction of Welham marshalling yard, L & NWR, near Market Harboro, opened 1 July 1904. It was still in Strachan's stock at the sale of his last contract in May 1913 at Red Wharf Bay, Anglesey, L & NWR, and was purchased by Jees Hartshill Granite and Brick Company Limited for their 2ft 6½in gauge system at Hartshill, near Nuneaton, Warwickshire. It survived there, named *Butcher*, until scrapped in 1945. It is likely that the standard gauge Hunslet locomotive was not included in the sale as Strachan still had a locomotive of the same description on later contracts and in any case the Tanat Valley contract was still in progress at the time of the sale. It seems certain that the W & L had no interest in the contractors' stock at the sale and one can only assume that the other two narrow gauge locomotives (*Strachan No 8* and *Hunslet 307*) left for pastures new.

PRUNING THE STOCK LIST

The W & L minutes of 19 December 1900 record agreement with the Cambrian Railways, as future operators, for the following stock to be available for the opening of the W & L at a total estimated cost of £6,350:

2 locomotives	£3200
2 coaches	£ 900
1 extra coach	£ 200
40 wagons	£1000
4 covered wagons	£ 240
2 cattle wagons	£ 170
1 travelling crane	£ 150
10 timber trucks	£ 250
2 'break' vans	£ 240

Mr H. E. Jones, locomotive superintendent of the Cambrian Railways, was given responsibility for preparation of designs for the stock. These were submitted in January 1901 with a recommendation that the crane be excluded if the W & L board had to make further economies. Possibly because of the dual interests represented by the Cambrian Railways and R. Y. Pickering & Co Ltd, the rolling stock builders of Wishaw, Lanarkshire, two sets of drawings exist of rolling stock designed for the opening of the line. In view of the current interest in 'what might have been', the outline drawing of the unbuilt design (probably by Pickerings) for a proposed coach is reproduced on page 150. In addition, on page 160 there is a preliminary design by Beyer Peacock of a locomotive with a smaller boiler than that which was actually built. The Cambrian Railways made strenuous efforts to persuade the W & L board to include a third locomotive in the estimates (together with a small shed at Llanfair to house it), but lack of capital precluded this and the orders actually placed were:

June 1901 to Beyer Peacock & Co Ltd, Gorton Foundry, Manchester.

2 locomotives at £1,630 each.

October 1901 to R. Y. Pickering & Co Ltd, Wishaw, Lanarkshire.

3 coaches, 40 wagons, 4 vans,
2 cattle vans, 2 brake vans, at a total cost of £2,477.

The provision of timber wagons, rather surprisingly, was deferred. This stock was to form the backbone of the railway for the whole of its commercial existence, being supplemented only by a few timber wagons, cattle vans and sheep wagons, the latter being rebuilds of original open coal wagons. There seems no evidence that proposals to try transporter wagons to carry standard gauge wagons over the branch were ever carried out, but an index to Cambrian wagon drawings does indicate that a transporter wagon was designed for the w & l line.

MOTIVE POWER

1 *The Earl* 0–6–0 side tank, Beyer Peacock, 3496/1902, arrived 2 September 1902.

1923 renumbered GWR 822. Name removed 1951.

2 *The Countess*, Beyer Peacock, 3497/1902, arrived 30 September 1902.

1923 renumbered GWR 823, renamed *Countess* in 1930. Name removed 1951.

These two identical locomotives were designed by Mr S. E. Garratt, of Beyer Peacock & Co Ltd, and supplied for the opening of the line. The makers' illustration of No 2 appears on page 108. Beyer Peacock were not light railway specialists and their design for the w & l is not without interest. In view of the ruling gradient of 1 in 29, and the fact that similar reverse gradients were encountered at Golfa summit and at Coppice Lane (see gradient profile), it was necessary to have a short boiler to minimise the risk of uncovering the crown of the firebox. Presumably to obtain maximum adhesion an 0–6–0 wheel arrangement straddling the firebox was adopted

Page 143 *ROLLING STOCK – 2*

(above) *No 2 brake van as rebuilt by* GWR *in use as temporary booking office at Sylfaen, 1964;* (below) *cattle van at Messrs Pickering's works, 1902*

Page 144 NEW ERA

Page 144 *NEW ERA*

(above) *No 10* Sir Drefaldwyn *waits with a Llanfair-bound train at Sylfaen, the terminus from 1972 to 1981. A lengthy run-round loop was constructed and it has formed a useful passing place for the Welshpool service;* (below) *in preparation for the re-opening to Welshpool, No 7* Chattenden *starts the descent of Golfa incline on a crew training run in 1981. The rear entrance cab is a W&L modification*

—this resulted in a very long rigid wheelbase (10ft 0in) considering the severe curvatures on the line. Almost certainly a light railway specialist would have favoured an 0–6–2 type with short rigid wheelbase, even at the expense of higher total weight. The engines had outside frames, outside cylinders and valve chests with Walschaerts valve gear. Although this was new to the limited British narrow gauge light railway scene, it was not novel as has often been claimed. For several years British manufacturers had been supplying this arrangement on narrow gauge locomotives for colonial light railways and for industrial service at home.

The numbers 3496/7 are carried on the motion but not on the builders' plates. They are re-issues of numbers originally allocated in 1892 to 4–4–2 tanks for the Buenos Aires Great Southern Railway which were never built.

Leading dimensions of W & L *Nos 1 and 2, as built:*

Cylinders	11½in diameter by 16in stroke
Boiler barrel	7ft 0in long by 3ft 5in outside diameter
Length over buffers	19ft 11½in
Width over footplate	6ft 9in
Firebox (outer)	2ft 9in by 3ft 10½in
Firebox (inner)	2ft 3in by 3ft 4½ in by 3ft 7¼ in high
Tubes	119 tubes 7ft 6in long by 1¾in outside diameter
Heating surface	Tubes: 396sq ft Firebox: 37sq ft Total: 433sq ft
Grate Area	7½ sq ft
Wheel diameter	2ft 9in
Water (side tanks)	350 gallons
Working pressure	150lb
Weight (tare)	17 tons
Weight (working order)	19 tons 18cwt
Tractive effort (85% wp)	8175lb

Vacuum and handbrakes were fitted, acting on all wheels. In order to clear the ashpan the trailing wheel brakeblocks acted from the rear end, the other blocks acting from the front end. Steam assisted sanding was fitted, the sandboxes being tucked between the boiler and the tanksides. Ramsbottom safety valves were mounted over the firebox. A small bell mounted on the cab roof was intended to act as a warning at road crossings and over the Welshpool town section. Traverser jacks were usually carried on the footplating over the valve chests.

Both engines survived the Cambrian era without major modification and this is some indication of the success of the design. Former drivers of these locomotives in original form pay tribute to their sturdy construction, but it seems that the boilers were not very free steamers and an inordinately long wait was often necessary to raise steam from cold. The steam sanding gear, a Beyer Peacock feature, was unsatisfactory under light railway conditions. Sand which is damp or of the wrong grade can be relied upon either to clog up the outlet or be blasted clear of the rails altogether! On such a severely graded line this was a serious deficiency. Although the steam valves are still fitted, the controls to the cab have been removed from both engines.

The Great Western influence was soon evident by the fitting of huge safety valve casings of the familiar Swindon brass 'trumpet' pattern. Oswestry men say these were adapted from casings formerly on old 'single-wheelers' and subsequently stored at the works. More important was the fitting of steam heating equipment to warm up the long suffering customers. Probably this coincided with replacement of the original tiny rectangular front buffer beam by a deeper version recessed top and bottom, as this would have facilitated attachment of the extra piping. This steam heating piping was removed from No 1 by 1956 but remained on No 2 until 1964. By the late 1920s the original boilers were due for renewal and in 1929 The Earl was sent to Swindon Works for an extensive overhaul. A new boiler and copper firebox was fitted of similar dimensions to the original boiler but with 136 tubes, $1\frac{5}{8}$in outside diameter and 7ft $3\frac{1}{4}$in long, the total heating surface being thereby increased to 457sq ft. The external appearance of the locomotive was greatly changed by standard GWR boiler fittings, including a parallel chimney topped by a copper cap (replacing the original tapered stove-pipe), top feed apparatus, a very large steam dome and, inevitably, the safety valve 'trumpet'. Twin whistles, incorporating the deep 'emergency' whistle, were also fitted. Swindon's concern for aesthetic appeal was evident enough in the fine finish of their express locomotives, but the appearance of Great Western rebuilds of engines from absorbed lines often left much to be desired. It was, therefore, perhaps just a fortunate accident that all the incongruous fittings on the rebuilt *Earl* added up to a most pleasing effect. Certainly in the affectionate attitude which was to surround the narrow gauge after the 1939-45 war, the chunky and slightly pre-

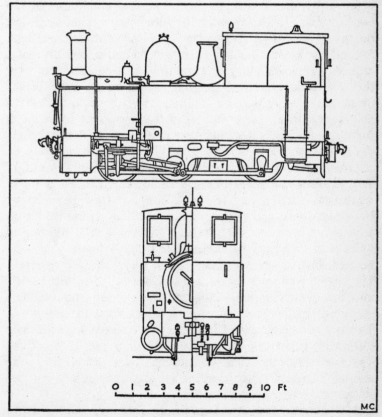

No 2, *The Countess* as running 1971, showing GWR boiler fittings

posterous proportions of the W & L engines were to have an appeal all their own.

Following the return of 822 in 1930, 823 was sent to Swindon in July of that year for similar treatment. No further major modifications were carried out by the GWR, but extremely ugly deflectors were fitted to throw smoke and steam from the safety valves clear of the cab windows. This problem had been aggravated by extending the cab forward to enclose the whistle valves.

During the 1939-45 war the engines received only minimum maintenance, though 822 did get a general overhaul at Swindon in March 1942. By the end of 1946 both were in very poor condition, with badly corroded fireboxes, worn tyres and generally run down mechanical condition. Of the two, 823 was in the worst state with 77,000 miles since last overhaul, and on 10 December 1946 she was declared unfit for further service. Consequently 822 had to soldier on alone, reduced to the indignity of a monthly boiler inspection, until the intended closure of the line could be effected. In the event this was not possible and major repairs could be delayed no longer. On 21 November 1947, 823 was sent to Swindon for a major overhaul including a new firebox. Unfortunately the strain was too much for 822, which failed completely on 28 November 1947 so stopping all services. As a result of very efficient mobilising of resources, a remarkable amount of work was carried out at the Welshpool shed between 30 November and 4 December 1947, including removal of all wheels for returning of tyres at Oswestry works, refitting of axleboxes, overhaul of motion, repairs to brake gear, and replacement of several boiler tubes, stays and flange rivets. The engine was ready to resume services on 5 December 1947, an effort which earned a congratulatory letter from Swindon —the authorities had estimated fourteen days for the work. This is a good example of how the W & L was able, with main line facilities on call, to survive with only two locomotives. There is evidence that an attempt was made to locate another locomotive for the line in 1947, apparently without success.

823 returned from Swindon on 15 February 1948 and 822 was sent away eleven days later, returning on 26 June 1948.

Thus the line was then provided with two locomotives put into first class order at considerable cost, and this was to prove a key factor in decisions to maintain services for several years. By February 1956, however, both engines were again unserviceable. 822 had to go to Oswestry Works on 10 February for re-tubing and tyre turning and was away until 15 March, no services being possible between these dates. 823 was completely out of action with a loose axle crank and was destined never to run again under BR auspices. She was sent to Oswestry for storage on 16 March 1956. This left 822 to operate the final months and to clear the line of wagons and equipment after closure in November 1956. After this 822 languished in the Welshpool shed until sent to join 823 in Oswestry Works on 7 May 1958.

Liveries

The makers' illustration shows No 2 specially painted in lined works grey for photographic purposes. When turned out new both engines were in the standard Cambrian Railways livery of the period—gloss black, lined middle chrome yellow with a fine lining of signal red on each side of the yellow band. After 1910 the broad lining of the W & L locomotives is reputed to have been changed to pale straw (or off-white). Brass nameplates with red painted background were centrally mounted on the tank sides and oval plates carrying the running number and the full light railway title were affixed to the upper cab sidesheets.

The makers' plates were mounted on the side of the smokebox. During the latter part of the 1914–18 war an austerity livery of plain grey is recalled by old employees. Under Great Western ownership both engines soon acquired Swindon green, unlined. The W & L company numberplates were removed and the nameplates transferred to the cab sidesheets. Because of the restricted space available the nameplates The Countess were abbreviated to Countess by the simple expedient of hacking out the offending letters and brazing the remainder together again! Full size cast iron Swindon numberplates, including the magic initials GWR, were put at the centre of the sidetanks and 'G W' gold shaded transfers were applied, one each side of the numberplate. In the 1939–45 war both engines became unlined black, but after nationalisation *Countess* reverted to unlined green. The letters 'G W' were erased from both locomotives and a small 'w' appeared below the 823 numberplates to emphasize Western Region ownership. A curious nonsense was the Oswestry (89A) shedplate affixed low down on each smokebox door. Following an alarming increase in the activities of souvenir hunters the nameplates were sent to Swindon for safe keeping in March 1951, but the numberplates were carried until after closure, being sent to Swindon in January 1957.

The Wickham Trolley (GWR No PWM 1906)

In 1940 Messrs D. Wickham & Co Ltd, of Ware, Dorset, supplied a new four-wheeled inspection trolley to the line. A small shed in Welshpool yard, off the 'main line', was used to house the machine. The trolley was Wickham No 2904, type 8s, and seated four persons on back to back seats. These seats folded down to facilitate loading into the train should this be necessary. A 350cc blower-cooled J.A.P. engine was fitted,

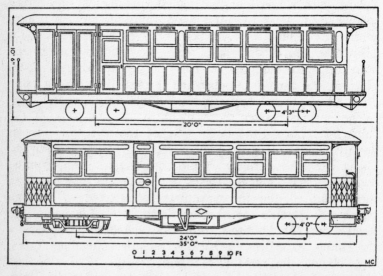

(*above*) Proposed composite coach (Pickering drawing No 1707). (*below*) Composite coach, as built 1902. Note limited luggage accommodation

power being transmitted through a cone type clutch. Main dimensions when new were: Length overall 5ft 3in (later increased to 6ft 11in by large footboards), width overall 3ft 7in, height overall 4ft 2in, or 3ft 1in with the seats folded down. Wheelbase 2ft 8in, wheels 1ft 6in diameter. The trolley survived to be taken over by the preservation society.

COACHES

W & L GWR

No.	No.	Type	Class	Built	
1	6338	Bogie Composite	1st/brake/3rd	Pickering	1902
2	6466	do.	do.	do.	1902
3	4154	Bogie saloon	all 3rd	do.	1902

These three coaches supplied by R. Y. Pickering for the opening of the line were the only passenger stock operated on the w & l for the period of public passenger services 1903–1931. All were impressive bogie vehicles with steel frames 35ft 0in long over headstocks. The bodies were 6ft 6in wide and the height from rail to rooftop was 10ft 0in; the bogies were of 'American' pattern, with disc wheels 1ft 11in diameter at 4ft 0in wheelbase. Vacuum brakes were fitted, with handbrakes on the balconies. The saloon bodies were constructed of oak and mahogany, 30ft 0in long, with a covered balcony added at each end. These balconies had lattice gates and two wooden steps for easy access as there were no raised station platforms on the line. The guard could pass from coach to coach via gates and fallplates arranged to span between the balconies, but passengers were not permitted to use these or, indeed, to travel on the balconies at all while the train was in motion. Having regard to the grossly inadequate accommodation reported on some fair days, however, one can imagine that here was one rule that was occasionally stretched. The third class seats were lathed, only the first class having simple mat 'upholstery' and the luxury of floormats.

Nos 1 and 2 were composite coaches having a small first class compartment for 10 persons, a guard's compartment near the middle (fitted with a brake wheel) and a third class compartment for 26 persons, a few of whom could have squeezed into a tiny 'smoking' sanctum. The compartments were separated by sliding doors with glazed upper panels. Infiltration of the first class by third class passengers was no doubt inhibited by the presence of the guard in his den between them! The provision for luggage and 'smalls' traffic was minimal and it was soon evident that the goods brake van had to be attached to all passenger trains to supplement the space for this traffic. The alternative design for the composite coaches, shown on page 141, had a distinct section for luggage. No 3 was an all-third class saloon seating 46 persons, only 16 of these being accommodated in the 'smoking' section.

The coaches were originally fitted with oil lamps but when taken over by the GWR No 3 had already been fitted by the Cambrian with acetylene gas equipment. In October 1923 all three coaches were fitted by the GWR with their incandescent gas equipment charged from cylinders at Welshpool. The Cambrian management were notorious devotees of the metal footwarmer, filled with hot water at the start of the journey, and it was left to the GWR to bring the delights of steam heated coaches to the W & L.

With the cessation of passenger services in 1931 the coaches were railed to Swindon Works and stored off bogies in the paint shop until scrapped in 1936. This delay has been said to be due to thoughts of using the bodies on the Vale of Rheidol section of the GWR. There is a strange sequel to this tale as there still exists a Swindon drawing dated 1931 which infers that the bogies were to be modified for use in the 'River Dee Bridge reconstruction'!

Coach liveries

The full Cambrian Railways livery was applied to the new coaches. The lower body panels were bronze-green, the upper panels and waistline white (varnished off-white), with mouldings picked out in red and yellow. The underframe was black, edged with a fine red line. The coach number appeared within a garter emblem all in gilt and centrally placed below the waistline, with the W & L company's monogram displayed at the same level towards each end. (From early photographs it seems that this monogram was not repeated when the coaches were repainted.) The class was boldly lettered along the waistline in gilt. Unfortunately this splendid livery was short-lived, as in 1909 economies included the adoption of an all over bronze-green coach livery. In due course this drab guise was applied to the W & L coaches.

Soon after GWR control, the lower and upper panels were painted in the familiar chocolate and cream colours of that railway, the GWR monogram taking the place of the gartered number at the centre of the lower panels. The GWR number was painted in a conventional position at the end of the waistline and the letters GWR placed at the centre of the waistline immediately over the monogram.

GOODS STOCK

First described is the original Pickering stock of 1902, with subsequent developments in chronological order.

The 1902 Pickering stock

W & L Nos	Type
1 and 2	Brake vans
3 to 6	4 ton closed Goods Vans
7 and 8	closed Cattle Vans
9 to 48	4 ton open wagons

These were all 4-wheeled timber framed vehicles. Chapter 3 has already referred to the difficulties regarding coupling gear. Most of the stock, including the goods and brake vans, was delivered without side chains but following reports from Strachan that wagons on loan to him were breaking couplings, Denniss flatly told the W & L board in December 1902 that he would not work the line without side chains on all stock. There was little option but to agree to this sensible demand, even at 17s 6d (87½p) per set of four chains! Pickering's official print shows that van No 8, at least, was delivered new with chains, as of course was all later stock.

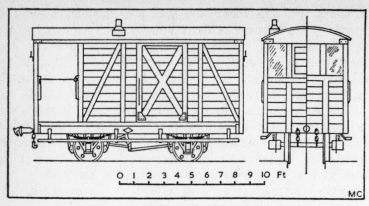

Brake van as first rebuilt, circa 1903

The Brake Vans appear to have been designed for use on goods (as opposed to mixed) trains. There was an open balcony at one end with only a drop bar to serve as door. From the balcony a plain boarded door led into the van which housed a stove, centrally placed, and a brakepillar (surmounted by a small control wheel) offset towards the balcony end. Two lockers also served as seats. Six-leaf springs were fitted, and brakes acted on all wheels but no sanding gear was provided. Even before the opening it was clear that these vans would have to serve on the mixed trains. Their scope would thus be greatly enhanced by provision of side doors to improve the miserable accommodation for 'smalls' traffic in the passenger stock. In April 1903 Oswestry Works completed drawings for provision of 3ft 6in wide sliding doors giving a 3ft opening on each side, the interior space being cleared by moving the stove towards the balcony and opposite the brakepillar. These modifications were carried out soon after the official opening of the line. Between 1905 and 1922 both vans were further modified, the van body being extended to cover the area of the former open balcony. The sliding doors just referred to were removed, but in compensation access to the van was by sliding doors in place of the former drop bars. The brakepillar was moved to a position between the doors. Through vacuum piping was added but there was no actual vacuum brake on the vans, the purpose of the fitting being solely to enable the van to be sited between the engine

and passenger coaches and so enable shunting to be minimised
in the absence of goods wagons. The sanding gear now fitted
was probably added at this time.

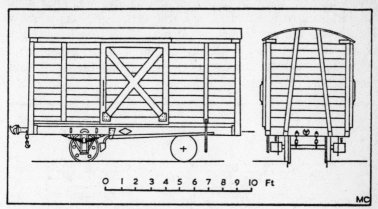

Goods van as built, 1902

The Goods vans were simply constructed in oak, clad with
white pine, with a sliding door each side to give a 4ft wide
doorway. The braking gear was simple in the extreme—a brake
handle on one side only acting on one wheel! Enthusiasts for
detail should however note that the original crude lever
shown above was later modified on all wagons to the improved linkage shown in the cattle wagon drawing below.
Six-leaf springs were fitted.

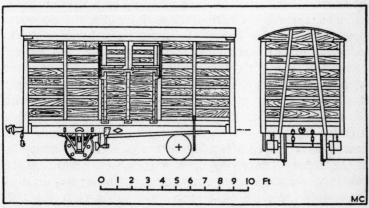

1902 cattle van, with modified brake gear

The cattle vans, similar in design to the goods vans, had slatted sides and ends and hinged drop doors to afford an easy access slope for the animals. The official capacity was seven animals. Some of the lower slatted area was later filled in. Pickering original drawings (ref. 2164 and 2194) show both goods and cattle vans as 9ft 0in rail-rooftop height. The goods vans still exist with this height and there seems no evidence to support statements elsewhere that the goods vans were at any time 10ft 0in high.

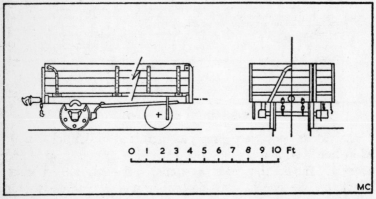

Standard open wagon. (*left*) As built, 1902 (Pickering drawing No 2087). (*right*) As modified: springs fitted and body later rebuilt by GWR

The open wagons as built were devoid of bearing springs, the frame-axlebox spacing being taken up by a wooden block. The effect of this on both track and freight was no doubt soon revealed, and as early as February 1904 Oswestry Works had designed new axleguards to take axleboxes and six-leaf springs. All wagons were so modified, probably by 1906 if the axlebox cover dates are a good guide. The wagon bodies were of white pine, four planks giving 2ft 1in inside height, with full length drop doors. The brakegear was similar to that fitted to the goods vans. Originally the side planking was secured with curved strapping with an inverted-V strapping on the ends. All surviving open wagons were rebuilt by the GWR with vertical straight strapping. Certain wagons, detailed below, were rebuilt into a form more suitable for the conveyance of sheep, cattle and timber.

Stock supplied after the opening

Private owner wagons have always been rare on British narrow gauge lines apart from the early tramroads, so it was an unusual development when in August 1903 Messrs Pickering designed an open wagon for Messrs J. Lloyd Peate and Sons, Coal and Lime Merchants of Llanfair. Although the main dimensions were identical to the W & L opens, there were several detail differences, principally (a) only a 3ft 0in middle section of the side was arranged as a drop door, (b) the side strapping was straight, (c) the wagon was the first open type on the W & L to be designed with bearing springs and (d) Wood's Patent axleboxes were fitted. Eventually five of these wagons were built—Peate numbers 2, 5, 6, 7 and 8 (the missing Peate numbers were filled by standard gauge wagons). The livery was maroon, with the owners' name lettered boldly in white. The Cambrian Railways fitted 4-ton registered plates. The wagons were scrapped at Llanfair in 1935—a registered plate from No 2 (Cambrian 601/1903) was dug up in Llanfair yard in 1970.

Timber Bolster Wagons (W & L Nos 49 to 54): There was much discussion in 1903 regarding provision of timber trucks for the line. When H. E. Jones of the Cambrian Railways wanted further remuneration before proceeding with the contract, the W & L sent director W. Forrester-Addie to Pickerings' works in Scotland. He discussed designs for an ordinary truck without either bearing springs or centre couplers. On

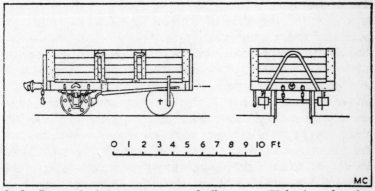

J. L. Peate & Sons' wagon, as built 1903 (Pickering drawing No 2613)

the builders' advice, when ten wagons were ordered, the specifications included these fittings and safety chains too. In April 1904, six trial bolster wagons were received. The order for the remaining four was cancelled in May 1906. The wagons followed in the style of the earlier stock, with wooden frames and the single brake handle acting on one wheel only. All of these wagons were converted to small four-planked open wagons by the GWR at Oswestry Works in 1946. By this time, timber traffic had virtually ceased.

Sheep Wagons (W & L Nos 10, 16, 17, 19, 24, 27, 36, 37): In February 1911, the Cambrian Railways accepted terms to convert six open wagons for carrying sheep or other livestock. The conversion cost £18 10s (£18.50) per wagon. Two further wagons were later converted, so that the GWR inherited a total of eight sheep wagons in 1923, recorded by them as having the above W & L numbers. Essentially they were flat wagons fitted with removable slatted sides and ends which fitted into sockets at the edge of the floor. The doors were fully planked, dropping to form a ramp for easy access, and the official capacity was 25 sheep. By 1956 GWR Nos 34163, 34172 and 71619 (W & L Nos 16, 19 and 27) had six-plank sides, the others only five planks. This could be due to the open cattle wagon conversions carried out on these wagons and referred to below. In later years, at least, sheep wagons were usually stored at Cyfronydd station loop.

GWR built closed Cattle Vans (GWR 38088, 38089): These vans were built in December 1923 at Swindon Works (Lot 914) for the Vale of Rheidol Railway. It seems that authority realised immediately that the Rheidol line in fact had no cattle traffic, and 38088 was regauged and sent new to the W & L. Curiously, 38089 was actually sent to Aberystwyth and after years of disuse it was returned to Swindon, regauged and sent to the W & L in April 1937. In general the outline of these wagons closely resembled the 1902 cattle vans, but the sturdy steel frames and steel body framing set a new standard for the W & L. The brakegear was unusual. The two brake-levers, one to each side, were unconnected, each lever acting on only one brakeblock, a duplicated form of the 1902 arrangement. After closure 38088 became the only ex-W & L vehicle to survive away from the line. (see Chapter 8).

GWR built Timber Bolster Wagons (GWR 17349 to 17354):
Built at Swindon Works in June 1924 (Lot 928), these were a
steel framed version of the 1904 bolster wagons. Following a
decline in timber traffic four of these wagons were rebuilt at
Oswestry Works in 1946 to four-planked open wagons, as
were all the earlier batch. This left only 17349 and 17353 as
timber wagons on the W & L (but see footnote to Appendix 9
re 17349).

*GWR open Cattle Wagon conversions (GWR 34143/63/72,
71584, 71619/87/99)*: To cope with increasing cattle traffic,
seven wagons were strengthened by lining the sides of the
interior with sheets of corrugated iron, a cheap and rapid
solution to the problem. In March 1930 three former sheep
wagons (34163/72, 71619) and three former open wagons
(34143, 71584, 71687) were so fitted, sheep wagon 71699
following in September 1937. Most of this cladding was
removed during the war years.

*GWR conversions to Open Wagons (GWR 8514 to 8516,
8518/21/23) (17350 to 17352, 17354)*: These were the ten
conversions from timber bolster wagons already described,
the official conversion date being 5 September 1946.

Wagon liveries

The original goods stock was painted in the Cambrian
Railways style. Bodywork was grey, roofs white and all ironwork black excepting tyres which were picked out in white
when new. Lettering was bold, in white, usually comprising
the title 'W & L', the capacity and tare weight of the vehicle.
The W & L opens, the Peate wagons and the 1904 timber
wagons bore a painted number on the ends when new. A cast
oval numberplate carrying the full title of the WLLR was
carried on the mainframe of wagons and vans. Originally
the brake vans had vermilion ends, an unusual feature which
was soon discontinued. The GWR first adopted a darker grey,
and then from about 1936 medium brown. Roofs were dark grey
or black. The earlier style of large 'G W' lettering on the sides
of vans and wagons was changed by the war years to small
lettering and numbers all on the left hand of each side. One
exception was that goods van numbers were on the doors.
The small style lettering was continued by British Railways.

Axleboxes

The goods stock used four different types of axlebox at various times, each easily identifiable by its coverplate. The 1902 open wagons had plain bearings with an unmarked coverplate. When springs were fitted to these wagons the new axleboxes were lettered 'W & LR' and usually dated between 1904 and 1906. All the 1902 vans, the 1903 Peate wagon No 2 (at least) and the 1904 timber wagons had oil boxes having a small valve over the bearing to feed lubricant. These are dated, clearly lettered 'Wood's Patent' and with the patentee 'Patent Axlebox Co Ltd' also shown. Finally, the GWR designed boxes for use on both the W & L and the Vale of Rheidol line. These are marked 'GWR 6 X 3 W & L V R'. Only the 1902 unmarked boxes may no longer be seen in service.

Pre-1956 stock dimensions

See Appendix 8 for dimensions when new.

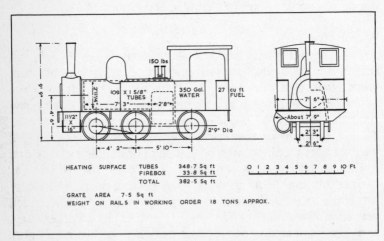

Preliminary design by Beyer Peacock for W & L locomotive

CHAPTER EIGHT

Locomotives and Rolling Stock after 1956

THE PRESERVATION ERA

With its objective of running a public passenger service from Welshpool to Llanfair, the problems of the new preservation company were formidable. The stock actually available consisted of the old w & l freight wagons and vans lying almost derelict in Welshpool yard and the two original locomotives mercifully stored at Oswestry Works. There was no other public passenger line in Britain of 2ft 6in gauge from which equipment could have been sought and the line had no repair facilities to enable extensive rebuilding or regauging to be contemplated. Even the w & l wagons, with their side drop doors, were unsuitable for ballasting work, as with the doors down it was difficult to get the ballast anywhere near the track! All in all it was a pretty grim picture—in retrospect it seems that only the mixture of good fortune and persistence which has so often favoured the Welsh narrow gauge has enabled the problem to be tackled in spite of acute shortage of capital.

In view of the contrary situation existing on some other preservation schemes, it should perhaps be made clear that all the locomotives and rolling stock listed below are the property of the w & l Preservation Company Limited, with the exception of the non-revenue-earning locomotives Nos 5 and 8.

Locomotive and rolling stock liveries (General note)
Soon after the formation of the preservation company, the decision was taken to adopt the Cambrian Railways livery throughout. This would have meant lined black locomotives,

bronze-green and white coaches, grey freight stock and black buildings with white window frames. In some degree this policy was implemented, as for example the repainting of *The Countess* at Oswestry in 1962 and the repainting of the coaches in 1965/6. After a few seasons of public services, however, it was increasingly realised that this livery was hardly suited to a line which in truth was in the entertainment business. Accordingly, it was decided that while *The Countess* would remain in Cambrian black, the other stock would be repainted in more colourful styles. In general this has led to other appropriate liveries being perpetuated, as with *The Earl* and *Monarch*, while the Austrian coaches can be seen almost exactly as they were in their home country.

MOTIVE POWER

W & L No	Name	Type	Builder	Acquired
(12)	–	four-wheel inspection trolley	Wickham built 1940	1959
(14)	–	four-wheel Austin trolley	Pres. Coy. built 1961	1961 (scrapped 1966)
1	*The Earl*	0–6–0 side tank	Beyer Peacock 3496/1902	1961
2	*The Countess*	0–6–0 side tank	Beyer Peacock 3497/1902	1962
3	*Raven*	four-wheel diesel	Ruston & Hornsby 170374/1934	1961 (sold 1974)
4	*Upnor Castle*	four-wheel diesel	Hibberd 'Planet' 3687/1954	1962 (sold 1968)
5	*Nutty*	0–4–0 geared (vertical boiler)	Sentinel 7701/1929	1961 (loan-returned 1971)
6	*Monarch*	0–4–4–0 side tank	Bagnall 3024/1953	1966
7	*Chattenden*	0–6–0 diesel	E. E. Baguley built 1949	1968
8	*Dougal*	0–4–0 side tank	Barclay 2207/1946	1969 (loan)
9	*Wynnstay*	0–6–0 diesel	Fowler 4160005/1951	1969 (sold 1972)
10	*Sir Drefaldwyn*	0–8–0 side tank	Franco-Belge 2855/1944	1969
11	*Ferret*	0–4–0 diesel	Hunslet 2251/1940	1971
12	*Joan*	0–6–2 side tank	Kerr Stuart 4404/1927	1971
14	*SLR 85*	2–6–2 side tank	Hunslet 3815/54	1975
15	*(JR No 5)*	2–6–2 side tank	Tubize 2369/1948	1983

The main objective in the motive power field was, of course, purchase of the two original W & L locomotives lying in

Oswestry Works, but the condition of the track was such that some engines had to be obtained at once to enable clearance work to proceed, as the steep gradients precluded hand-pushing of loaded wagons. It transpired, therefore, that the first three motive power units were modest internal combustion machines.

No 12 (Wickham trolley)

This vehicle, referred to on page 150, was taken over by the society and subsequently transferred to the preservation company. When acquired in 1959 the J.A.P. engine then fitted was worn out and attempts were made to replace this with a large motor cycle engine which happened to be available. Without doubt the resulting performance would have been hair-raising and perhaps fortunately it was realised that the frame was not strong enough to take the extra stress —in the end a much more suitable 350 cc J.A.P. engine was fitted. Even then the trolley was capable of a remarkable turn of speed and its soft springing gives a tendency to heel over on sharp curves—this is not transport for the faint-hearted! In 1967–8 the trolley was completely rebuilt without major structural alterations and is now used occasionally for inspection purposes.

No 14 (Austin trolley)

In an attempt to provide much needed motive power, a four-wheeled trolley was constructed by members of the company. The basis of this vehicle was a derelict hand pump trolley in Welshpool yard. From the appearance of the axles this had originally been a standard gauge vehicle later adapted for use on the w & l. A frame was constructed of steel angle and a 10hp Austin engine mounted to drive the wheels through the chain drive of the pump trolley. It was soon evident that the chain drive was inadequate and alterations were made by Hudson Engineering Co Ltd, of Welshpool, the trolley being returned complete on 11 March 1961. Two gearboxes were fitted, each with four speeds and reverse, but one box could only be operated by prior removal of the driver's seat! At first this vehicle was a definite asset though the complete absence of springs gave a very sporty ride, particularly as the speedy nature of the trolley was completely at variance with the sharp curves on the line. On two occasions the leading axle fractured—the second time was in early 1962 when the trolley was in full flight down Golfa bank and its unfortunate crew were projected into the nearest ditch. After this wiser councils prevailed and the trolley was never used again, being cut up at Heniarth in September 1966. The two trolleys were allocated numbers in the wagon series, No 13 being a hand trolley. It is however doubtful if these numbers were actually carried—certainly the Wickham bore only its small PWM 1906 plate by 1964.

No 3 Raven

Built in 1934 for the Mid Lincolnshire Ironstone Company at Greetwell, Lincs., by Messrs Ruston & Hornsby Ltd, of Lincoln, this was a standard 16/20hp four-wheeled cabless diesel locomotive, makers' No 170374. It was transferred to Nettleton Top mines, near Claxby, Lincs., in 1935. In 1944, John Lysaght Scunthorpe Works Ltd took over and eventually donated the locomotive to the preservation company. Delivery was made by road to the line on 28 March 1961. Three days later it ventured to Welshpool and thus became the first true locomotive to be operated by the new regime. One brass nameplate was fitted on each side of the bonnet together with W & L No 3 plates.

This robust little engine proved invaluable for maintenance work at a critical time in the railway's development, though after 1964 its use was limited by driving sprocket wear. In December 1966, the wheels and balance weights from Ruston 191680 built 1938 arrived from Nettleton Top and were transferred to *Raven*. In 1969/70, *Raven* was completely rebuilt incorporating a reconditioned engine from Belton Brickworks, Lincs. Despite renovation, however, this elderly diesel was of limited use in view of its low weight and on 26 October 1974, it was sold to W. Free, Frampton-on-Severn.

No 1 The Earl (ex B.R. 822)
No 2 The Countess (ex B.R. 823)

These locomotives were put to store by British Railways at Oswestry Works after the 1956 closure (see chapter 7). They stood side by side in the wheel turning bay off rails and without name or numberplates. In 1960, they were offered to the preservation company for £654, but it was not until 28 July 1961 that No 1 was unloaded from a well wagon in Welshpool yard by the Salop steam crane, thanks to a donation of £350 by one member of the company.

As received from Oswestry, *The Earl* was in grey undercoat but later in 1961 a plain black livery was applied. This was described at the time as 'temporary', yet it lasted until summer 1966 when a change was made to fully lined GWR green. Under preservation company auspices, both 822 and 823 reverted to their original titles under Cambrian operation with *The Earl* and *The Countess* nameplates centrally sited on the sidetanks and replicas of the *W & L Nos 1 and 2* plates on the upper cab sidesheets. At times the numbers have also appeared on the buffer beams.

822 was in quite good general condition when purchased, but 823 was in a run down state. Before it left Oswestry to join 822, various repairs were effected including re-tubing the boiler. The livery of 823 was Cambrian black, rather prominently lined straw and it made a brave sight when unloaded at Welshpool yard on 6 October 1962. After eight years' trojan service, *The Countess* was withdrawn in need of a heavy overhaul. This started in 1978 and gradually fittings and plating throughout were refurbished and renewed where necessary.

The biggest problem lay with the firebox. Funds were raised and in 1985 the boiler was moved to specialist contractors at Warrington to have new crown stays fitted and wasted rivets replaced as well as being retubed. At last, in July 1985, the locomotive returned to service and ran very successfully for over twelve months. Disappointingly, further work was then necessary to remedy leaking firebox seams.

Meanwhile, *The Earl* worked until 1978 when it became apparent that here, too, major repairs were needed, including new firebox crown stays. Then an offer from the National Railway Museum, York, to house and display the locomotive seemed a better alternative than open storage in Llanfair yard. A further move took place in 1987 to the Birmingham Railway Museum.

No 4 Upnor Castle
Built by F. C. Hibberd in 1954 to their 'Planet' design, this was delivered to the Admiralty, Lodge Hill and Upnor Railway,

Kent, numbered *Yard No 44*. The frame was of H-section girders and each axle was chain driven. A Type FD6 Foden engine was fitted developing 126bhp at 2,000rpm but derated to 105bhp at 1,800rpm.

Following the closure of the Upnor line the w & l were able to purchase the engine which arrived at Welshpool by road on 21 February 1962. Nameplates *Upnor Castle* were fitted at a naming ceremony at Llanfair on 22 August 1962. Admiralty representatives were in attendance, the name having been suggested by the Admiralty. Numberplates *W & L No 4*, of similar style to those on the steam locomotives, were fitted and the *Yard No 44* plate removed. The dark green livery, fully lined in white, was not altered while the loco was at Llanfair. No 4 performed a most valuable function as principal motive power for the maintenance trains from 1962 to 1968, but its short wheelbase led to rough riding. This was accentuated by the curious weight distribution, especially the very heavy buffer beams which encouraged yawing at only moderate speeds.

In 1968 the opportunity arose to obtain the six-coupled diesel formerly on the Upnor line, and to finance the purchase of this locomotive (which became No 7) *Upnor Castle* was sold to the Festiniog Railway, where it has been regauged and considerably rebuilt to suit that line's loading gauge. This is probably the first instance of the sale of a working locomotive between two preservation lines. *Upnor Castle* left Llanfair for Portmadoc on 13 February 1968.

No 5 Nutty

The London Brick Company Limited had 2ft 11in gauge lines in the Fletton district of Huntingdonshire, some equipped with geared steam locomotives of special design to work within a six foot loading gauge in the brickworks. The last survivor of these was *Nutty*, built by the Sentinel Waggon Works Limited, at Shrewsbury, in 1929 (Works No 7701), being employed until 1964 at Hicks No 1 works alongside the Great Northern main line. By arrangement with the Narrow Gauge Museum at Towyn it was brought to Llanfair by road on 28 June 1964. *Nutty* has the usual Sentinel features—a vertical water-tube boiler, chain drive and twin cylinders, in this case mounted horizontally to reduce height clearance. During the 1964/5 winter the locomotive was overhauled and regauged to 2ft 6in at Llanfair, the sole external alteration being the fitting of Chattenden couplings to the rear end. The unlined bright yellow livery was continued. After steam tests on 8 February 1965 it was used primarily as a maintenance train engine, having insufficient braking power for passenger working over the heavier grades, though it was seen on occasional turns to Heniarth in 1965 during the emergency period following the Banwy Bridge collapse.

While *Nutty* proved to be a reliable machine, the very cramped cab was hardly suitable for double manning. The gauge glasses, for instance, are but a few inches from the fireman's face. After 1966 it was rarely used and on 23 October 1971 it was finally sent to the Narrow Gauge Museum Trust at Towyn, Merioneth.

No 6 Monarch

This locomotive was built by W. G. Bagnall Limited of Stafford in 1953 (Works No 3024), and was the last narrow gauge steam engine to be built for ordinary commercial service in the British Isles. Messrs Bagnall had been the established supplier of steam motive power to the extensive 2ft 6in gauge system of Bowaters Lloyd Pulp and Paper Mills Limited at Sittingbourne, Kent, and in 1950 they offered their 0-4-4-0 articulated side tank design to Bowaters to enable heavier trains to be hauled over the long viaduct at the southern end of the line. This design had been introduced in 1936 for sugar estate work in Natal, South Africa and it was possible to demonstrate that the double bogie arrangement offered considerable advantage in weight distribution on the viaduct. The original enquiry for two locomotives was reduced in 1952 to a firm order for just one. No 3024 finally emerged from the builders on 31 July 1953, painted the then standard Bowaters livery of medium green lined red, with black frames and brass nameplates *Monarch*, appropriately commemorating the Coronation of Queen Elizabeth II in that year.

Monarch has power bogies in the reversed position, that is with the cylinders at the inner end and with steam connections via Flextel ball joints of modern design feeding inside admission piston valves. In view of repeated assertions that the engine is of Mallet type, it is necessary to point out that this is not so. Both bogies are free to swivel, whereas the Mallet has the rear power unit integral with the frames. *Monarch* is in fact a modern version of the Meyer type.

The mainframes, which carry the side tanks, roomy cab and bunker, are of rolled steel channel with cross bracing to carry the bogie pivot mountings. The boiler has an 8-element superheater. Perhaps the most unconventional feature on a locomotive of this size is the steel marine (ie circular) firebox, widely used by Bagnall in their smallest contractors engines but here no less than 5ft 9in long! While this type of box is regarded as inferior to the common types for locomotive work, in this case it has the big advantage of giving adequate clearance under the rear bogie for pipework and the like. There is an added bonus of very cheap construction and replacement costs as the minimum of stays is required. Fittings when new included steam and handbrakes acting on all wheels, four sandboxes, British Detroit hydrostatic lubricator, and a large spark arrester chimney.

It cannot be said that *Monarch* was a great success at Sittingbourne. There were several teething troubles, principally connected with the firebox, and it was not until the tubes were welded into the firebox tubeplate in 1957 that the locomotive was capable of the intensive and arduous service required. After renewal of the firebox in 1961, the engine worked successfully until taken out of service in May 1965, as first stage of economy measures which were ultimately to close the commercial operation of the Bowaters line in 1969.

Thanks to the generous co-operation of Bowaters, the w & l was able to purchase the engine, together with a large stock of spares. At this time the preservation company was recovering from the financial setback resulting from the Banwy Bridge collapse, and the costs of the acquisition of *Monarch* were donated by a member. After a repaint it left Kemsley Mill by road on 6 May 1966, arriving at Llanfair two days later. Standard *W & L No 6* plates were fitted on 21 May 1966.

Monarch ran on trial later that summer but did not

see passenger service until August 1973, after a major overhaul which included retubing, new wheels and the fitting of a stovepipe chimney.

Various problems made it necessary to undertake an extensive programme of work including modifications to the grate which improved its steaming performance. *Monarch* worked again in 1976 and spasmodically until autumn 1978 when it failed with a recurrence of weeping tubes and defective superheater flues. Repair work began yet again but in due course it was decided that resources could not be spared for this problematic locomotive.

No 7 Chattenden

This engine was built by E. E. Baguley Limited of Burton on Trent, Staffordshire, to the order of the Drewry Car Company Limited of London, and carries Drewry serial number 2263. Delivered new to the Admiralty, Lodge Hill and Upnor Railway, Kent in November 1949, it was originally titled *Yard No 107* and later became *Yard No 58*.

In contrast to the Planet locomotive (w & L No 4), it has plate frames, six wheels with outside coupling rods and jackshaft drive to the rear pair of wheels. A Gardner 6LXB engine was fitted in 1980, derated to 150bhp, with a maximum governed speed of 15mph. Drive is transmitted via a fluid coupling to a 4-speed epicyclic gearbox with self-changing gears, final drive to the jackshaft being through a David Brown spiral bevel. Flameproof equipment includes 12v lighting and an exhaust gas scrubber

When the Upnor line closed the locomotive was moved to Ernsettle Depot, near the Saltash Bridge, Devon, and in 1965 was transferred to Broughton Moor Depot, Cumberland. At neither site did it do much work, the wheelbase being too long for the sharp curves in the depots. When the engine was declared surplus in 1968 it was purchased by the w & L, arriving at Llanfair by road from Broughton Moor on 13 February. The nameplates *Chattenden* fitted in May 1968 recall the earlier title of the Upnor line—the Chattenden and Upnor Railway. *Chattenden* has proved to be a most useful and reliable machine, capable of taking in emergency a five coach passenger train and yet having well designed controls for shunting work.

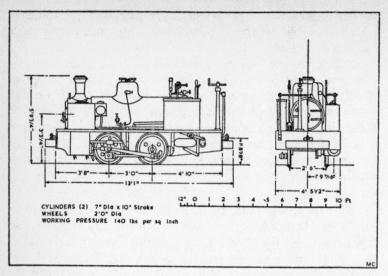

Barclay No 2207, as built 1946 for Glasgow Corporation

No 8 Dougal

This locomotive was built by Andrew Barclay, Sons and Co Ltd, of Kilmarnock (Works No 2207) and delivered new in July 1946 to the Provan Works of Glasgow Corporation Gas Department. The design dates back to 1903 when six engines of the type were supplied to the newly opened Provan Works. The use of miniscule steam locomotives has distinguished many Scottish city gasworks, but only the relatively modern Provan site used the 2ft 6in gauge. The squat appearance was due to the very limited confines of the gasworks retort house. Barclay 2207 was operated for most of its working life at Provan with its brake gear completely removed(!). The Provan system closed on 25 May 1958. Several of the surviving engines were scrapped and it has been reported that Barclay 2207 was sent to Abercrombies local scrapyard in error in 1961. Happily it was recovered and rescued for preservation by the Railway Enthusiasts' Club at Farnborough, Hants, leaving Glasgow by rail on 23 March 1962. Unfortunately the R.E.C. was not able to carry out its plans for the engine and so it was sold to two W & L members in a partly dismantled condition for eventual service at Llanfair. On 18 November 1967 it left Farnborough for Oldbury, Worcs., for overhaul, where it remained until again moved by road to Llanfair on 8 November 1969. When fully restored it was put on permanent loan to the preservation company. Necessary alterations to enable the engine to work on the w & l include larger water tanks, increasing capacity from forty to eighty gallons, and fitting new handbrake gear to the original design. No 8 was first steamed at Llanfair on 19 December 1975.

When turned out new, Barclay 2207 was painted standard Barclay olive green, with painted title *Provan Works No 1* and the full Glasgow coat of arms surmounted by the letters *G.C.G.D.*, all on the little coal bunkers. In 1969 maroon livery was adopted, and standard *W & L No 8* plates and *Dougal* nameplates were later fitted. The name has no profound significance—just a doggy cartoon character with a similar low chassis to the Barclay.

No 9 Wynnstay
This locomotive links the w & l with the exotic railways of East Africa. Not only is it structurally almost identical to the East African Railways 8000 class, apart from gauge, but No 9 itself was built for the ill-fated Groundnuts Scheme in 1951 by John Fowler & Company (Leeds) Limited, Works No 4160005. After the collapse of the groundnuts project it remained on the builder's hands until sold about 1954, with two similar locomotives, to the British Portland Cement Manufacturers Limited at Lower Penarth Works, Glamorgan, becoming their No 5. The 2ft 6in gauge system here was abandoned in 1968, and in 1969 the w & l purchased No 5, the most complete survivor, with many spares, including the engine unit and set of wheels of No 3 (Fowler 4160006). The locomotive was moved by road via Brecon and Newtown on 9 August 1969. Livery became Iona green (BS6/074), darker than at Penarth, with yellow lining. *W & L No 9* and *Wynnstay* plates were fitted on 16 May 1971.

W & L No 9 has a McLaren type M4 four-cylinder engine developing 100bhp at 1100rpm. A heavy duty dry plate clutch transmits the drive to an integral 4-speed and directional gearbox. The jackshaft drives the middle pair of wheels by a lengthy connecting rod. Unfortunately, the rather inflexible engine, manual clutch and gearbox made the locomotive unsuitable for passenger operation over the severe grades. On 18 March 1972, it left for the Whipsnade & Umfolozi Railway at Whipsnade Zoo.

No 10 Sir Drefaldwyn

This Continental o–8–o side tank is of modern construction but few British locomotives of any age have such an interesting history. It was built by Société Franco-Belge at their Raismes works, France, Works No 2855, and supplied to the German Military Railways in March 1944. As built, it was an o–8–o tender locomotive with short auxiliary side tanks, Feldbahn type KD11. Many of these locomotives were built for use on the war fronts, particularly the Eastern Front. The original design was German, and the drawings surviving for this locomotive are by Berliner Maschinenbau A.G. at their Kleinbahn works, Berlin.

Fortunately much of the original documentation concerning the engine's history has been recovered. From this it appears that it was at the Feldbahn stores depot at Mittersill, near Zell-am-See, Austria, when this fell into the hands of the American Occupation Forces at the end of hostilities. On 6 January 1946 it was loaned to the Salkzkammergut Lokalbahn, near Salzburg, though there is some suggestion that it was not used until boiler test formalities were completed in August 1946. Built to German standard 750mm gauge, trouble soon ensued on pointwork and adjustment to correct 760mm gauge was carried out. The SKGLB purchased the engine as from 1 April 1950, working it on the picturesque Salzburg—Bad Ischl line as No 19 until July 1955 when it was sold to the Steiermärkische Landesbahnen (Styrian Government Railways) near Graz, Austria, for use on the 42km line from Weiz to Ratten. It was rebuilt in 1957 with full length side tanks and a coal bunker to replace the tender, the result being an increase in adhesive weight from 22 to 27 tons in working order. The bunker is built on an extension of the frames with the original buffer beam left in position. The engine was numbered 699–01, probably because its original tender form was identical to the Austrian State Railways 699 class, resulting in two locomotives numbered 699–01 in Austria. In 1961 the original steel firebox was replaced by copper and 699–01 worked regularly from 1962 to late 1965, when steam working on all the Steiermärk lines was much reduced.

In general design this engine gives an insight into modern Continental narrow gauge practice. The boiler has the quite high working pressure of 200lbs/sq in, and is fitted with a 3-row 16-element superheater supplying steam through piston valves to cylinders of 'oversquare' proportions. Perhaps the chassis is the most novel feature to British observers—the four axles are arranged to give a total wheelbase of only 8ft 10½in compared with 10ft 0in for the *three* axles of *The Earl*. In addition the front axle has an arrangement to allow lateral movement on curves and the third pair of wheels is flangeless, the net result being a very compact unit capable of negotiating sharp curves with ease. The nominal tractive effort (at 85 per cent working pressure) is 13,535lb which must make it a contender for the most powerful engine of its size to work in Britain. Steam, vacuum and handbrakes are fitted, the vacuum equipment operating on the train only, not on the locomotive wheels. A steam turbogenerator is mounted alongside the chimney, powering twin headlamps at front and rear and maintenance lights beneath the side-tanks.

699–01 left Weiz depot on 4 December 1969 and arrived at Llanfair on 11 December. Details of negotiations and the journey appear in Chapter 6. The cost of the project was £1,200, entirely met by members' donations. Following a trial run on 1 May 1970, the new acquisition made its debut on special trains for members on Saturday 2 May 1970—the first occasion in the railway's 67 year history that the *Earl* and *Countess* had been supplanted by another steam locomotive on the Castle run. After minor adjustments, No 10 went into regular service proving a very economical machine which steams well on slack coal—a fuel which Nos 1 and 2 are very loth to digest! It is intended that the Steiermärk livery will be adopted, i.e. black, lined red. As the result of a ballot of members, the company chose the name *Sir Drefaldwyn* (Welsh: Montgomeryshire) and the official naming ceremony was held on 5 September 1971. A cast of the Montgomeryshire crest is mounted above the nameplate.

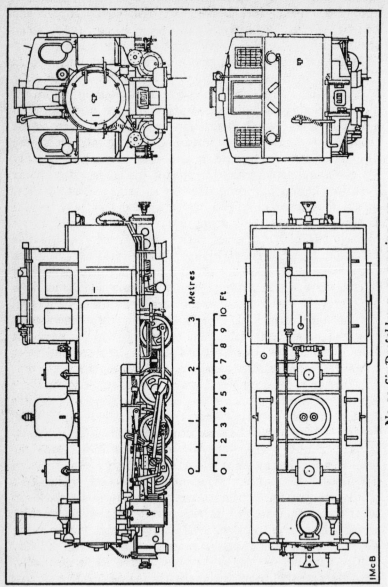

No 10 *Sir Drefaldwyn*, as running 1971

IMcB

No 11 Ferret

This was one of the earliest mines diesels built by the Hunslet Engine Co Ltd, Leeds. Built in 1940, Works No 2251, this flameproof locomotive is fitted with a 50hp Gardner 4L2 engine. It has four wheels with outside coupling rods and jackshaft drive to the leading pair of wheels. A deep well in the cab gives the crew adequate room despite the low overall height. Until 1970, the engine worked as *Yard No 86* at the Admiralty armament depot, Dean Hill, near Salisbury, Wiltshire, being acquired by the W & L from a dealer's yard. The costs were met anonymously by a member and the machine was delivered by road to Llanfair on 11 July 1971. It has since proved very successful on engineering trains.

No 12 Joan

During the 1970s, the Preservation Co made two interesting additions to the fleet of passenger locomotives. *Joan* is an 0-6-2 side tank built by Kerr Stuart & Co Ltd, of the California Works, Stoke-on-Trent (Works No 4404) and sent new on 24 September 1927 to the Antigua Sugar Co, British West Indies. The engine worked there until 1956 after which it was rarely used due to dieselisation of the system. In 1971, it was purchased by the W & L from the Antiguan Government Estates and Development Board and shipped via Georgetown, Guyana, to Liverpool, completing its journey of over 4,000 miles to Llanfair on 27 November.

Kerr Stuart 4404 was the maker's standard Matary class chassis, modified to take a larger than standard Huxley class boiler, presumably to give more steam for the heavily graded 'main lines' of the sugar system in Antigua. As built, the working pressure was 160 lb/sq in giving a tractive effort of 7555lb at 85%. The original water tanks carried 420 gallons. Over the years, the large firebox has been used to burn a variety of fuels —at first oil was used but during the 1939–45 war a shortage of oil led to the use of coal or sugar cane waste (bagasse). In 1949–51, the engine was extensively renewed above footplate level, with a new boiler, steel firebox, full length side tanks, all from the Hunslet Engine Co, Leeds. The engine returned to service in 1951 for only a few years before being put in store.

After arrival in Wales, No 12, as it was to become, was

stripped down for a detailed examination and minor modification to suit operation on the w & l. Originally, two Mumford vertical steam feedpumps had been fitted on each side of the front footplating but by 1971 the left hand pump had been replaced by a large horizontal pump on top of the sidetank. This pump was removed in favour of a standard injector, and in 1983, the right hand pump was similarly replaced. Other work carried out included retubing, conversion of the left hand oil bunker for coal, fitting of vacuum brake equipment, removal of various buffer beam girder appendages used in Antigua to carry tools (and personnel!), fitting of Grondana couplings, adding safety chains and an extensive rebuild of the cab with a closed back.

A steam turbogenerator was fitted in Antigua to power typical American Baldwin searchlights but the closed back of the new cab necessitated a change to a Sierra Leone Railway searchlight at the rear. The engine was put into regular service on 10 April 1977 painted Midland Red, unlined, and numbered 12. The large nameplate *JOAN* was retained. With its large balloon style chimney, *Joan* is a very good example of the colonial estate machine, once a major feature of the British locomotive industry.

No 14 Sierra Leone Railway 85

This is a 2–6–2 side tank locomotive with outside frames built by the Hunslet Engine Co, Leeds, in 1954. It was the last of 32 similar engines built by them for the Sierra Leone Railway between 1898 and 1954. The first six of these had 10in by 15in cylinders, but from 1903 the larger boilered 10¾in by 15in design was established as a standard which survived for over 50 years with only minor modifications. These engines were designed for quite long journeys (the slr main line was over 200 miles long), and in later years they banked trains from the Water Street terminus through the main streets of Freetown.

The last order for two of the class was placed in May 1952 by the Crown Agents for the Colonies. These became SLGR 84 and 85 and cost £21,273 for the two. They were sent whole from Leeds on 8 October 1954 to Liverpool for shipment to Freetown. They had Walschaerts valve gear, a flush roundtop firebox, Ross pop safety valves and 5mm Gresham & Craven combination injectors mounted on the firebox backplate. Steam and handbrakes applied to the engine with a vacuum ejector to operate the train brakes. Sandboxes fitted between the tanks and the boiler (like *The Earl* and *The Countess*) and, uniquely to these two locomotives, Timken roller bearings were fitted to the pony trucks. By 1975, No 85 had lost the rear roller bearing pony truck in a swap of trucks.

The locomotive arrived at Llanfair via Liverpool on 7 August 1975 having been shipped with the four coaches acquired by the w & L. Not surprisingly, considering the complete abandonment of the SLR, the machine was in a rather rundown condition and a thorough overhaul was necessary. After complete dismantling, it was evident that much replating was required particularly in the areas of the smokebox sides, the bunkers and the rear pony truck support plates, which had apparently been damaged in some long forgotten mishap. The extra coalboxes fitted forward on top of the sidetanks were deemed unnecessary and were removed, greatly to the benefit of the engine's appearance. After reassembly, a mid-green livery was used, being a former livery of the SLR and a *No 14* plate affixed. The oval *SLR 85 1954* plate was retained on the tank sides. The engine therefore appeared much as a 2–6–2 tank working in Sierra Leone before the 1939–45 war.

No 14 entered regular service at Easter 1979 and has proved to be a reliable performer, giving a smooth ride with free steaming characteristics and economy of fuel. Certainly it is a testimony to a long lived design.

No 15 (ex-Jokioistenrautatie no 5)

The original home of this locomotive was the 750mm gauge Jokioisten Railway (Jokioistenrautatie) in southern Finland. This 14 mile link with the main line ran through gently rolling farmland to the industrial town of Forssa. Opened in 1898, the line's heyday was in the 1920s although there were hectic times in World War II. A shortage of motive power was highlighted at the end of the war when the JR lost a 2–6–2 Henschel tank locomotive to the USSR as part of Finland's reparations. It was therefore decided to order two identical side tank locomotives to handle heavy trains of transporter wagons, timber and passenger traffic on this undulating line. The design was for 2–6–2 machines with outside frames and boilers giving 527 sq ft of heating surface enhanced by 161 sq ft of superheating elements—boiler power superior to any locomotive on the W & L.

The contract was undertaken by the Tubize division of the Société Anonyme Les Ateliers Metallurgiques at Nivelles in Belgium. The second of these to be completed, in 1948, became JR No 5.

The closure to passengers in 1954 saw No 5 confined to freight duties and then, after a working life of only fifteen years, it was withdrawn with the firebox needing major repairs, never to run again in Finland. The end almost came in 1972 when closure of the line was imminent and No 5 was offered for sale for scrap. Fortunately, a well wisher in England bid for it and, being unexpectedly successful, then faced the daunting task of collecting his prize! Not uneventfully, it was eventually landed at Harwich only to languish for a decade in store in East Anglia. In 1983, it was purchased by the W & L and delivered by road to Llanfair on 28 September.

The aim was to guarantee the continued preservation of an impressive example of continental locomotive building. The nominal tractive effort (at 85% boiler pressure) of 11,720 lbs should make W & L No 15 a formidable performer in its new home, the particularly large driving wheels being powered by cylinders of massive proportions (for the narrow gauge). However, full restoration and operation remained a low priority task. Work was limited to external renovation, mainly involving painting in an attractive livery of mid-green, lined in red.

ROLLING STOCK

Apart from the original W & L stock, which was renumbered on acquisition, it has been the policy to retain the running number of the former owner of both coaches and wagons, unless duplicate numbers would result.

(a)   ex British Railways (W & L section) stock.

W & L No		BR No	Type
	1	8759	Brake Van
(*orig 4)	2	8755	Brake Van
(*orig 6)	3	38088	Cattle Van
(*orig 2)	4	100664	Covered Van
	5	allotted to Cattle Van 38089 (see below)	
(*orig 3)	6	100666	Covered Van
	7	71794	4 ton Open Wagon
	8	71738	4 ton Open Wagon
	9	34159	4 ton Open Wagon
(*orig 5)	10	71692	4 ton Open Wagon
	11	34154	4 ton Open Wagon

With the exception of wagon 11, all this stock was obtained from British Railways in 1959 and removal from the graveyard in Welshpool yard was effected by horse power in September of that year. It was soon discovered that Cattle Van 5 had been sold in error and that in fact it was the property of the Festiniog Railway which had purchased it earlier, apparently for conversion to a bicycle van. It lay in Castle station loop until early 1962 with the wheels removed and then the body was taken on a flat wagon to Welshpool for rail transit to Minffordd. The FR ultimately rebuilt it into a stores van of very changed appearance. Wagon 11 was recovered from the standard gauge yard at Welshpool on 17 August 1960, necessitating the laying of temporary track across the yard followed by lifting and carrying the wagon by crane to the existing narrow gauge line at the far end of the Cattle Market yard.

The wooden frames of most of these wagons were in poor condition, particularly the opens which in any case were not very suitable for ballasting work. Inevitably, these became neglected in the early years of passenger working. Despite the little use they received, two of them had broken frames by 1969 and there was a distinct danger that the original W & L wagon might become a thing of the past. To prevent this calamity a programme of recovery was started in 1970. Two wagons (Nos 7 and 9) were condemned for spare parts.

* these numbers carried 1959-60.

Wagon 10 was rebuilt in 1971 with new wood throughout, including a frame to the original pattern and by July 1973, wagon 8 had also been restored.

Cattle Van 3 is rarely used, except as a weed-killing unit. On the other hand the brake vans and the covered vans are the mainstay of the maintenance trains. It is at least arguable that the spirit of the old W & L still lives on as long as one can shelter round the stove in the brake van from the worst of the Mid-Wales winter.

(b) ex Admiralty (Lodge Hill & Upnor Railway) stock

Upnor and W & L No.	Type	Builder	Date Built	Date of arrival
32	10ton low sided wagon (bogie)	Cravens Ltd Sheffield	1942	28 July 1961
33	do.	do.	1942	28 July 1961
35	do.	do.	1942	28 July 1961
38	do.	do.	1942	28 July 1961
41	do.	do.	1942	28 July 1961
60	10ton high sided wagon (bogie)	do.	1942	25 Nov 1961
65	do.	do.	1942	25 Nov 1961
196	Toastrack coach (bogie)	do.	1941	28 July 1961
199	do.	do.	1941	28 July 1961
200	do.	do.	1941	25 Nov 1961
204	do.	do.	1941	25 Nov 1961
212	Brake van (four wheel)	do.	?	25 Nov 1961
213	Breakdown van (four wheel)	do.	?	25 Nov 1961
(214)	'Combination Car' (bogie)	D. Wickham & Co Ld, Ware. No. 7372	1957	25 Nov 1961

The arrival of the first batch of these vehicles coincided with the return of *The Earl* to the line in July 1961. The 30 ton Salop MPD steam crane was used to transfer both batches to W & L metals in Welshpool yard. All of this stock runs on Hyatt roller bearings.

The Toastrack Coaches seat forty persons, the transverse slatted seats giving five doorless 'compartments'. The wooden bodies were of two types—196, 199 and 200 had vertical boarding, tubular handrails and a roof of curved corrugated iron, while 204 had horizontal boarding, angle handrails and a boarded roof. The main dimensions of the two types are identical. The steel frames are carried on bogies of simple construction, and the manganese steel wheels have no separate tyres. Excepting 199, there was separate brakegear on each bogie, with brakelevers each side. A large vertical brakehandle on the side of the body of 199 acted on both bogies through a central brakeshaft. This brakehandle was removed about 1963. Considerations of comfort and safety led to reconstruction of some of the toastracks as closed coaches, 204 being tackled first as it had the simplest type of body to convert. The rebuild included full length doors made from old GWR corridor doors and fixed windows, but much of the original side boarding was retained The coach returned to service in 1963. The second conversion was 199. Here it was necessary to remove all the sides and replace with steel panelling and new door pillars. Sliding windows were also fitted. In 1966, when part rebuilt, the central brakeshaft was adapted to give a centre brake compartment in the coach, so providing a second much needed bogie guards vehicle. 199 was finally completed in 1968. However, being unsuitable for vacuum brake conversion, in November and December 1978, all four toastrack coaches were transferred to the Sittingbourne & Kemsley Railway.

The 'combination car', to use its official Admiralty title, was in railway terms a first/second/guards coach, and was formerly used to convey officers and NCO's. When received by the W & L it had no running number, the present one (214) being adopted in 1968. It was painted a darker green than the toastracks with white windowframes; in the centre of the sides was the badge of the Royal Naval Armament Supply Department with 'Upnor-Lodge Hill Railway' under it. In contrast to the spartan toastracks this is a rather splendid vehicle, with an all-steel flush panelled body, full length doors, sliding windows and upholstered seats in the small compartment. At one end is a well equipped guard's compartment with sanding gear, electric light controls, Klaxon horn and brake wheel. The passenger accommodation comprises a compartment for six and a saloon for fourteen persons. The preservation company fitted upholstered seats throughout and a supplement of one shilling (5p) was charged per single trip in this coach, this practice being discontinued from the 1968 season. The coach is carried on heavy bogies fitted with coil springs giving a very smooth ride.

The bogie low-sided wagons have steel frames, chassis and bogies very similar to the toastrack coaches, but the bodies are over a foot wider. All have single plank sideboards with arched endboards 2ft 3in high. In order to improve the utility of these wagons for ballasting work the endboards are being lowered to the height of the sideboards, excepting wagon 41 which is being retained in original condition.

The bogie high-sided wagons were formerly ammunition wagons with sides 3ft 7in over platform with two sets of double doors each side and arched endboards 4ft 8in high. Although the frames and bogies are similar to those of the low-sided wagons, the bodies are only as wide as the toastrack coaches so that the underframe is visible flush with the body sides. The W & L found these wagons of limited use and in 1969 the sides of wagon 60 were completely removed. This gave a flat wagon with high ends very suitable for sleeper transport.

Brakevan 212 is a small four wheel van with bench seats for up to ten persons and is fitted with a central pillar brake screw. In 1979, two of its four cast iron weights were removed and it was rebuilt as an enclosed van with sliding doors.

Breakdown van 213 has a similar chassis to 212, including the central brake pillar. Like 212 it has a cast iron block at each end forming massive sandboxes, but there are no supplementary iron blocks to boost the weight further. The body is a closed van, with double doors on one side only. The preservation company in 1963 made a double window in the other side, and in this form 213 became the regular guard's van (with 214) on the passenger trains until the more satisfactory bogie coach 199 was available with a guard's compartment in 1966. On the Upnor line 213 sported a broad yellow band painted horizontally around the waist of the body, no doubt to restrict its use to emergency duties only. It was repainted plain brunswick green by 1963.

(c) other ex Admiralty goods stock.

| 248 | 5-ton four-wheel flat wagon (ex Broughton Moor 212) |
| 249 | do.   (ex Broughton Moor 249) |

| 210 | four wheel brake van (ex Trecwn 11) |
| 211 | do.   (ex Trecwn 13) |

Wagons 248 and 249 arrived by road at Llanfair on 6 July 1968, having been stored in a Mossbay, Workington, scrapyard. Built as closed vans, they were cut down to flats before disposal by MoD. Brakevans 210 and 211 came to the w & L in October 1973, having run in a Pembrokeshire depot. They had a closed section with side doors and an open balcony with brake handwheel. 210 was rebuilt as a fully closed tool van in 1975. 211 saw little use and, in 1988, left to work elsewhere.

(d) ex Zillertalbahn, Austria, passenger stock.

W & L No	ZB No	Type	Builder .	Date Built
B14	B14	four-wheel saloon	Grazer W & M.F. A.G., Graz.	1900
B16	B16	do.	do.	1901
B17	B17	do.	do.	1901
B27	B27	do.	do.	1906
*572	*B25	do.	do.	1925

*later B24.

These coaches were donated to the preservation company by the zb as a culmination of several years of friendly relations.

B14, B16, B17 and 572 arrived at New Drive crossing on 11-12 April 1968 (see Chapter 6). Three of the coaches were original zb wooden bodied vehicles, the fourth being a steel bodied coach built new for the Salzkammergut Lokalbahn

(SKGLB). Historically these coaches are significant as being typical of many coaches of both types constructed by the Grazer Waggon und Maschinen Fabriks A.G., of Graz, Austria for most of the Austrian 760mm gauge lines. All coaches are on steel frames, the coupling gear at each end being joined by a rigid steel drawbar, the effect being that each coach 'hangs' on this continuous drawbar and coupling stresses to the coach mainframe are minimised. Simple vacuum brakes are fitted, as used on the ZB until 1967/8, though in earlier times 572 would have had compound vacuum gear on the SKGLB.

The original ZB coaches are B14, 16 and 17 (the prefix B is the continental convention signifying second class). B14 has the distinction of being one of the four coaches available at the opening of the very first section of the ZB in December 1900. It was built at Graz in 1900 as ZB 21, renumbered 14 in 1933. Two sixteen seat saloons have slatted wooden seats with a central gangway. The gangway is continued at each end via swing doors to outside balconies with drop plates to afford passage from coach to coach. These drop plates are not used on the W & L, however, as they are not considered safe enough for children. Electric lighting is fitted, operated

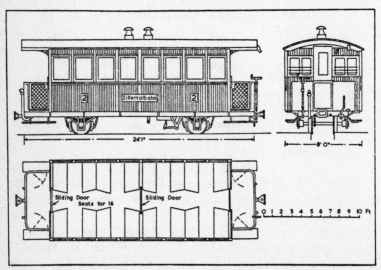

Ex-Zillertalbahn coach B17, as received in 1968

on the ZB from the locomotive. Steam heating pipes ran through the saloons.

B16 and B17 were built in 1901 and also renumbered in 1933. Coach B16 resembles B14, but has one undivided saloon with sliding doors while B17 has two 16-seat sections. By 1977, B17 was unfit for further service. After careful dismantling, the wooden body frame was renewed, section by section while new matchboard panelling and window frames were made. Five years of painstaking work were devoted to restoring B17 to its original condition. In 1988, B16 was scheduled for similar rebuilding.

B24 was bought by the Zillertalbahn in 1957. It was built for the SKGLB at Graz in 1925 in a batch of ten third-class coaches, later becoming No 572. Two saloons seat sixteen and twelve passengers, four places having been lost about 1947 to make a lavatory cubicle, converted in Wales to a guard's compartment. Electric light and steam heating were fitted, with individual transverse heaters under each pair of seats.

B27 arrived at Llanfair on 18 September 1975. Although of similar construction to B24, the ventilators over the windows belie a different history—before Zillertalbahn ownership it was No 3660 of the Austrian State Railway. The saloon is divided, 16 seats each section, there being no lavatory. Unlike the other ZB stock it was automatic vacuum fitted.

(e) ex Bowaters (Sittingbourne and Kemsley Railway) goods stock.

SKLR and W & L No	Type	Builder	Date built	Date of arrival
610	high ended bogie flat wagon	Butterley Co	1951	1 Dec 1978
631	do.	do.	1951	2 Dec 1978

These were standard all-steel Bowaters pulp wagons. During 1979 they were rebuilt, the high ends being cut down and three steel drop doors fitted each side. The resulting very effective ballast wagons were immediately used on the extensive ballasting on the Welshpool extension works.

(f) ex Sierra Leone Railway passenger stock.

These large steel modern style coaches, running on Timken roller bearings, are the last survivors of approximately 45 such coaches supplied by Britain to the Sierra Leone government on attaining independence in 1961 and formed the official last train on the SLR from Cline Town to Waterloo on 17 November 1974. As received, the third class coaches had longitudinal slatted seats while 1207 had 16 (insect infested!) armchairs. Three coaches have been re-seated using bus seats, capacity 50 passengers. The other (1040) was used initially as an exhibition coach in aid of the Welshpool Extension Fund. The lavatories have been removed from all the coaches but 1207, 1066 and 1048 have had the space converted to a guard's compartment with vacuum brake valve.

SLR and W & L No	Type	Builder	Date built	Date of arrival
1040	3rd class bogie coach	Gloucester C & W Co	1961	8 Aug 1975
1048	do.	do.	1961	8 Aug 1975
1066	do.	do.	1961	8 Aug 1975
1207	1st class bogie coach	do.	1961	8 Aug 1975

General note on coupling gear and braking.

Since 1963 a choice has had to be made between the original Norwegian ('chopper') type couplings (drawbar height 2ft 2in) and the link-and-pin couplings of the Upnor and Austrian stock (nominal height 1ft 10in). At an early stage the link-and-pin was selected and by 1970 most of the stock was so fitted but it was realised that a more rigid coupling was desirable when working to Welshpool. Fortuitously, it was possible in 1977 to purchase from Sierra Leone a complete set of Grondana couplings for the railway. These couplings, used also, for example, on the Ghana Railways, consist of a conventional screw link coupling mounted over sprung centre buffers (drawbar height 2ft 0in). By 1979, all passenger and freight stock in regular use were Grondana fitted. As a further essential step for operation to Welshpool, the fitting of automatic vacuum brakes to all passenger stock was proceeded with. Fully fitted trains commenced in 1977 and all coaching stock was fitted by 1979. These two developments greatly increased the standard of safety and smoothness of operation. The Upnor toastrack coaches were still fitted with link-and-pin couplings when sold.

The Upnor wagons were adapted to Grondana couplings by moving the couplings from the bogies to an extension of the main frames.

Rolling stock liveries (see general note on page 161)

Passenger stock. For the opening season of 1963 the Upnor passenger set was painted plain brunswick green, but by 1966 the set had acquired the Cambrian Railways livery—deep bronze-green lower panels, white upper panels with a gold waistline and black ends. The company coat of arms appeared on a metal plate centrally placed on each side. Following the policy outlined on page 162 the whole rake was repainted by 1968 in a new livery of cardinal red (BS1/025) lower panels, mid cream upper panels with a black waistline and black ends. The Austrian coaches were painted in the red-brown livery of the Zillertalbahn (except that for a time B24 appeared as 572 in SKGLB green) and this has continued to date. The SLR coaches, received in mid-green, were repainted red (BS 1/025) with a cream panel to surround all the window area. Black ends and grey roof complete the livery.

Goods stock. All goods stock is painted grey (BS9/097) with black ironwork and white lettering, so following the tradition of both the W & L and the Upnor lines. Vermilion ends have been restored to the brake vans.

Dimensions of the Preservation Company stock

See Appendix 6 (locomotives) & Appendix 7 (rolling stock).

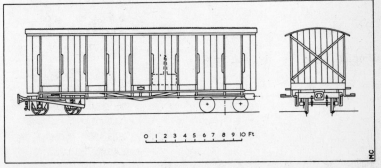

'Toast-rack' coach 196, as received from Admiralty, 1961

Appendices

I : STOPPING PLACES, CROSSINGS AND DISTANCES

Except where stated, passenger facilities were provided at stopping places from 4 April 1903 and ceased as from 9 February 1931. LC denotes level crossings.

		Miles	Chains	Altitude (ft)	Notes
Welshpool station		0	00	243	
Church Street	LC	0	22	–	
Brook Street	LC	0	34	–	
Seven Stars		0	35	264	
Standard Quarry		0	67	–	Mineral siding only
Raven Square		0	72	305	
	LC	0	77	–	
		0	78		Termination of Railway from 18.8.63
Welshpool (Raven Square)		0	79	–	Re-opened 18.7.81
New Drive	LC	1	46	–	
Golfa		2	66	557	
Cwm Lane	LC	2	68	–	
		2	99	603	Summit of line
Sylfaen Farm		3	53	554	Sylfaen Halt from 1.2.13. Reopened 6.6.64 to 6.9.64. Re-opened from 15.7.72
Coppice Lane	LC	4	34	578	
					Castle Caereinion—Llanfair Caereinion section reopened to passengers on seasonal basis from 6.4.63.
Castle Caereinion		4	62	538	
	LC	4	65	–	

Dolarddyn Crossing	5	35	470	Appeared as Halt in working timetable from July 1904 and in public timetable from 8.8.29. Not reopened.
Hydan Fawr LC	6	01	–	
Cyfronydd	6	57	381	
LC	6	58	–	
	6	68	–	Brynelin Viaduct
	7	44	–	Banwy Bridge
Heniarth Gate	7	54	360	Heniarth from 1.2.13
LC	7	55	–	
Dolrhyd Mill	8	34	365	No Halt shown on working timetables; used for a period prior to World War I—exact dates not known. Not reopened.
Water Tower	8	46	–	
Llanfair Caereinion	9	05	381	

2 : PERMANENT WAY

Except as noted below, the railway is laid with the original rail. It is flat bottomed, of 45lb to the yard and laid mainly in 30ft lengths with staggered joints. It was intended to use 75lb to the yard grooved rail for the crossings in Welshpool but Collins gained approval of the Board of Trade for the use of the same rail as elsewhere. Bearing plates are used and the rails fastened down with spikes, sometimes double on the outside. The Light Railway Order only required these double spikes at joints and on curves, and only if through-bolts or coach screws were not employed. On the mixed gauge section in Welshpool, chaired track was laid. Near Sylfaen, a short section was relaid some time after 1926 with approximately 56lb rail said to be from the Tanat Valley Light Railway. Check rails were laid in many places—on sharp curves, on bridges and on the steep Golfa bank. Some have since been lifted. Metal ties were also introduced at intervals on curves as required by the Order.

When the terminus was constructed at Raven Square in 1980, the incline out of the station was laid with new 60lb rail.

The railway was constructed with 6ft sleepers of creosoted

Baltic fir, 9in by 4½in, laid at 3ft intervals and ballasted with river gravel and broken stone about 5in deep. Re-laying has taken place at various times with cut-down standard gauge sleepers. Between Sylfaen and Welshpool, the preservation company has used 5ft 3in Australian jarrah wood sleepers (8¼in by 4½in) for long life having experimented with ex-London Transport jarrah sleepers on short sections elsewhere. Until 1978, the preservation company used recovered sleepers from British Railways, sawn in half and laid at approximately 2ft 6in intervals. Though the last of the track east of Raven Square has been lifted, the present administration managed to purchase much of the rail for future use. Under the original Order, no fencing was required for one mile from the commencement of the railway.

3: SPEED LIMITS AND SPECIAL REGULATIONS

Under the Light Railway Order of 8 September 1899, the maximum speed permitted was 20mph. Lower speed limits were required to be imposed in various places. Where the gradient was steeper than 1 in 50, the limit was 15mph; on curves sharper than 5 chains radius and where the line was unfenced between Welshpool terminus and Raven Square, it was 10mph—except that, in Welshpool, a lower limit could be imposed by direction of Welshpool Corporation.

Numerous speed restriction boards were erected along the nine miles of the line—in the up direction, Cambrian drivers had to watch for nine 10mph boards, two 5mph boards and three 4mph boards. The GWR introduced 15mph boards, too, and instructed drivers not to exceed 5mph over crossings within 76 chains of Welshpool station or 10mph over public level crossings.

By 1911, the overall speed limit had been raised to 25mph as the appendix to the Cambrian Railways Working Time Book for 1 June of that year shows. The date of the actual raising of the speed limit was probably earlier; it may be significant that journey times were reduced by 15 minutes in 1905. On 11 August 1927, an Extra Traffic Notice was published by the GWR which included an apparently new amendment to the instructions regarding the overall speed—it was reduced to 20mph. Some time prior to 1943, the speed limit was further reduced—to 15mph which prevailed until closure in 1956 and was reimposed when the line was opened again in 1963.

Special regulations were in force with regard to timber trains. Under the GWR, speeds were not to exceed 10mph. A match truck was required when round timber overhung two wagons, although if it was no longer than three wagons' length, two wagons were to be used connected by a drag chain attached at intervals to the timber.

The maximum loading height was 12ft. Owing to the steep gradients, regulations required shunting on the Standard Quarry siding and the Tanllan corner timber siding near Llanfair to be carried out with the locomotive at the Welshpool end. Eventually, regulations necessitated the collection of down traffic from the Standard Quarry *before* the morning train left Welshpool terminus —at the last-named place it had to be formed into the train. Drivers were enjoined to 'freely ring the engine bell' when approaching level crossings in Welshpool and to whistle when approaching all other crossings. The GWR did not permit the working of two engines coupled together.

When the railway opened, all sidings were worked by ground frames from the Isca Foundry and were opened by Annett's key attached to the train staff. At Castle Caereinion, points were worked from the signal box following its installation in 1907; the reintroduction of ground frames there seems likely to have been carried out round about 1931. Existing frames are from Tyer and Co Ltd.

For the one-engine-in-steam system when the line opened, a round wooden staff painted red was used. The staff in use in 1921 was T-shaped. The preservation company operates a divisible staff system. The staffs consist of painted metal bars each marked with the names of the two stations at the ends of the appropriate section. Possession of the staff permits a train or light engine to move in *either* direction within that section. Two tickets, which are also metal bars, are attached to each staff, one for each direction within the section. A ticket is used when a blockman requires a train to move away from the staff after first showing the driver the complete staff. A second train with the staff and the ticket attached for the opposite direction can then follow when the first train has cleared the section. For ease of handling, metal hoops are provided with the staffs and tickets. Annett keys, painted yellow, are carried separately. There are block posts at Castle Caereinion and, since 1967, at Cyfronydd, while Sylfaen was introduced after running was extended to Welshpool. Instead of block instruments and bells, trains are signalled by telephone. Within Llanfair station limits, movements are now controlled by a two-arm bracket signal, a starting signal and shunting signals. Welshpool (Raven Sq) is similar.

4: TIMETABLES

Extract from Cambrian Railways Service Timetable, October 1908 page 29
Welshpool and Llanfair Light Railway
(Narrow Gauge)

DOWN

		18	3	5	7	9	11	13
		Goods Mon Tues Wed	Goods Thurs Fris & Sats R	¶ Mixed	Mixed Mons except	Mixed Mons only	Mixed	Mixed
		am	am	am	am	pm	pm	pm
Welshpool Station	dep	5 5	5 5	8 10	11 45	12 45	3 55	7 5
Welshpool Seven Stars	,,	:	:	*	*	*	*	*
Raven Square	,,	:	:	*	*	*	*	*
Golfa	,,	:	:	*	*	*	*	*
Sylfaen Farm	,,	:	:	*	*	*	*	*
Castle Caereinion	,,	:	:	8 30	12 5	1 5	4 15	7 25
Cyfronydd	,,	:	:	*	*	*	*	*
Heniarth Gate	,,	:	:	*	*	*	*	*
Llanfair	arr	6 15	6 15	9 5	12 40	1 40	4 50	7 55

UP		2‡ Mixed Mon Tues Wed	4 Goods Thurs Fris & Sats R	6 Mixed	8 Mixed	10 Mixed	12 Pass	14
		am	am	am	pm	pm	pm	pm
Llanfair	dep	6 35	6 30	9 40	2 15	5 30	8 0	...
Heniarth Gate	,,	*	...	*	*	*	*	...
Cyfronydd	,,	*	...	*	*	*	*	...
Castle Caereinion	,,	6 55	...	10 0	2 35	5 50	8 20	...
Sylfaen Farm	,,	*	...	*	*	*	*	...
Golfa	,,	*	...	*	*	*	*	...
Raven Square	,,	*	...	*	*	*	*	...
Welshpool Seven Stars	,,							
Welshpool Station	arr	7 30	7 45	10 35	3 10	6 25	8 50	...

* Trains must stop at all stations to pick up or set down passengers.
§ On Llanfair Fairs, i.e., the first Friday in each month, No 1 will be run as a Mixed train, stopping at all stations.
‡ On Llanfair Fair Days No 2 will run as a Goods
¶ On Llanfair Fair Days No 3 [sic] will run 30 minutes earlier.
No 11 to convey not more than two wagons in addition to the Passenger vehicles.
On Mondays all Up and Down trains will stop at the Crossing at Dolarddyn to pick up or set down passengers to or from Welshpool. Passengers must take Cyfronydd tickets. Trains will also stop at Dolarddyn on other days for picnic parties.

5 : FARES & TICKETS

Fares

For many years during the passenger-carrying era, the single
third class fare from Welshpool to Llanfair was 1s 2d (6p)—
2s (10p) first class. There were also market ticket arrangements:
in Cambrian days there were cheap third class returns to
Llanfair on Saturdays from Welshpool and all intermediate
stations; and from stations along the line to Welshpool on
Mondays. For the full distance, the return excursion fare was
1s 3d (6p) for many years and in 1903 even half-day returns were
offered, at 1s (5p), on Wednesdays and Thursdays. Through
tickets were offered to and from some main line stations; at
times this arrangement included cheap third class return market
tickets to Llanfair on Saturdays and from Llanfair to Oswestry
on Wednesdays (3s 5d—17p), to Newtown on Tuesdays (3s 3d—
16p) and to Wrexham on Mondays (5s 5d—27p).

Season tickets were offered at standard Cambrian rates when
that Company was operating the line. For example a third class
twelve monthly season ticket from Welshpool to Llanfair cost
£5 6s (£5.30) in 1905. By 1922 it cost £5 3s 6d (£5.17½) for a
third class six monthly season ticket. After 1931, special excursions on the line were usually charged at 2s 6d (12½p) return.
The final trip before closure cost 3s 2d (16p). The preservation
company's charges for the return journey from Llanfair to Castle
were 2s 6d (12½p) in 1963.

Tickets

During the early years of passenger services, tickets were issued
from the booking office at the passenger terminus in Welshpool
and at Llanfair Caereinion, but later the booking office at Llanfair was closed. These tickets were standard Edmondsons similar
to the operating company's main-line tickets. In fact the W & L
Company's name did not appear but instead that of the Cambrian
Railways (abbreviated to CAM RYS) and later GWR. Full details
of the ticket history have not been clarified, but a little more is
known of the punch-type, tramway style tickets issued by the
guard in Cambrian Railways' days which seem to have been
peculiar to the line. Guards' duties included both the issue and
collection of tickets. The tram-type tickets issued en route were
divided into three columns. In the centre column was printed

the fare, class, single or return, name of the operating company and the conditions of issue. The left hand column showed the stages. On the 1d single these were:

Welshpool—Raven Square Golfa—Sylfaen Farm Sylfaen Farm —Castle Caereinion Cyfronydd—Heniarth Gate.

On the right hand side the stages were reversed. The tickets were punched to show the points between which the passenger was entitled to travel: on the back was carried an advertisement of a local trader. By 1917, the tickets were marked 'Revised Fare'. It has been recorded that 1d tickets were white and 11d tickets were blue with a red bar down the centre. Card dog and bicycle tickets were also issued by the guard, and were 'To any station on Welshpool & Llanfair Line'. Bicycle tickets were orange and cost 6d, becoming cream when the rate was increased to 9d. From 1923 to 1931, under the GWR, it is presumed that guards issued passengers with standard ladder-type rail-motor issues. Tickets were later needed for enthusiasts who were carried on special trips after the cessation of passenger services. In BR days single or double coupon special excursion type issues were used.

Under the present administration, Edmondson card tickets are issued at the booking offices. For many years, they were printed by Williamson's of Ashton, bearing the preservation company's name, and showing the destination but not the fare. Return tickets are marked 'and back' and half-fare tickets 'Child'. Various colours have been used from time to time and commemorative tickets have been issued for special events. Guards use a travelling ticket rack for passengers joining at intermediate stations.

6: DIMENSIONS OF LOCOMOTIVES OF THE PRESERVATION COMPANY

Loco	Cyls in	Wheels diam ft-in	Length (a) ft-in	(b) ft-in	Width (c) ft-in	(d) ft-in
1 *The Earl* ⎫ 2 *The Countess* ⎭	2.11½ × 16	2-9	17-11	20-0	6-9	7-0
3 *Raven*	–	1-4	9-9¼	11-8	3-10	3-10
4 *Upnor Castle*	–	2-0	14-2			5-9
5 *Nutty*	2.6¾ × 9	1-8	11-10	13-3	4-8	4-10
6 *Monarch*	4.9 × 12	2-0	23-7*	27-7	7-0	7-7
7 *Chattenden*	–	2-0	14-2	16-1½	5-4	5-9
8 *Dougal*	2.7 × 10	2-0	11-8	14-2	4-5½	4-5½
9 *Wynnstay*	–	2-4	17-1	19-7½	6-7	7-0
10 *Sir Drefaldwyn*	2.13 × 12¼	2-2¼	20-7	23-3	7-8	8-4
11 —	–	2-0	12-4	15-4	3-11	4-0
12 *Joan*	2.10 × 15	2-3(1-6†)	19-1	22-5	–	7-5
14 *SLR 85*	2.10¾ × 15	2-4(1-6†)	19-1	22-4	7-2	7-5
15 *(JR No 5)*	2.12½ × 17¾	3-1½(1-11½†)	29-2	—	—	8-1½

Notes: (a) Over buffer beam mainplates.
(b) Over buffers (link-and-pin type except Nos 12 & 14).
(c) Over tanks/cab (steam locomotives) or bodywork (diesels).
(d) Overall.
* No 6 has 6in bunker overhang over rear buffer beam.   † bogie wheels.

7: DIMENSIONS OF ROLLING STOCK OF THE PRESERVATION COMPANY

For ex-BR stock see Appendix 8

Coaches:	Length over: headstocks ft-in	body ft-in	Width over: body ft-in	'clearance' ft-in
14	24-1	18-3	7-11	8-1
16, 17	24-1	18-10	7-11	8-1
572	24-1	18-3	8-0	8-3
196, 200	–	23-11	5-6	7-6
199, 204	–	23-11	5-11	7-6
214	21-0	21-0	6-0	7-0
1040, 1048, 1066, 1207	43-4	40-0	7-3	7-9

Goods stock:				
32, 33, 35, 38, 41 ⎫⎭	–	23-11	6-7	6-7
60, 65	–	23-11	5-5½	5-10
212	11-1	11-1	4-8	5-4
213	11-1	11-1	4-8	5-2
248, 249	11-1	11-1	4-7	4-9

Notes: * in original condition with sides
† in original condition with ends
‡ 'clearance' width includes doorhandles, steps, eaves,
Upnor bogie vehicles have no mainframe 'headstock' as couplings
are on the bogie frames

Height ft-in	Wheelbase ft-in	Water gals	B.P. lb/sq in	Weight (working order) t-cwt	Tractive effort at 85% b.p.
10-0	4-2 + 5-10	350	150	c21-0	8175 lbs
4-9	2-7½	–	–	3-5	–
	4-6	–	–	c13-0 tare	–
6-0¼	3-3	80	230	6-0	'80 hp'
9-6	3-3 bogies at 15-0 centres	500	185	28-10	12737
10-0	3-3 + 2-9	–	–	12-7 tare	–
5-10	3-0	80	140	6-10	2430
10-6	3-6 + 3-6	–	–	c17-0 tare	–
10-6	2-7½ + 2-7½ + 3-7½	700	200	27-0	13535
6-4	4-0	–	–	c8-0 tare	–
10-6	12-6 (2-9 + 2-9)	530	170	c21-0	8027
10-5½	15-4 (2-9 + 2-9)	470	160	c21-10	8417
10-8½	21-4 (3-9 + 3-9)	900	184	33-10	11720

rail to rooftop ft-in	Height: body to eaves ft-in	rail to eaves ft-in	Wheelbase: rigid ft-in	bogie centres ft-in	Wheels diam ft-in	Weight (tare) t-cwt
9-1	6-7	8-6	12-1½	–	1-10	4-15
9-1	6-7	8-6	12-1½	–	1-10	4-15
10-5	6-6	8-10	12-1½	–	1-10	5-15
8-7	6-0	8-1	3-6	17-6	1-8	4-0
8-9	6-0	8-3	3-6	17-6	1-8	4-0
9-6	7-6	9-0	3-6	11-0	1-8	
10-1½	–	–	4-9	29-0	2-0	c12-0
clearance'.	Height: rail to platform	rail to eaves				
5-6	2-9		3-6	17-6	1-8	†3-10
(3-4 with lowered ends)						
7-6	2-9	–	3-6	17-6	1-8	*3-19
7-11	2-3	7-8	5-0	–	1-8	7-14
8-0	2-3	7-8	5-0	–	1-8	c4-10
2-4	2-3	–	5-0	–	1-8	

M

8: DIMENSIONS OF W.L.L.R. (1902-1956) ROLLING STOCK

These dimensions will facilitate scaling up of drawings appearing elsewhere in this
tion when built. Surviving

	Length over headstocks ft-in	Width overall (body) ft-in	Height overall from rail ft-in	Height floor from rail ft-in
Brake vans	14-0	5-10	9-0	2-9
after r/b by C. Rys	14-0	6-3	9-0	2-9
after r/b by GWRy	14-0	6-3	9-0	2-9
Goods vans	14-0	6-3	9-0	2-9
Cattle vans '03	14-0	5-10	9-0	2-9
Cattle vans '23	14-1	5-8	9-0	2-8
Open wagons	10-0	6-4	4-9½	2-8½
Peate wagons	10-0	6-4	4-9½	2-8½
Timber wagons '04	8-6	6-4	3-2	
Timber wagons '24	8-2	6-0		
Sheep wagons	10-0	6-4	6-9	2-9
Short opens	8-2	6-0	4-11	

Note: Overall dimensions *include* doors but exclude eaves and ironwork appendages
doorwidths marked* are the

book. The data have been taken from the original drawings and so represent condi-
items show no significant changes.

Height eaves from floor ft-in	Width of doors ft-in		Wheelbase ft-in	Wheels diam ft-in	Weight tare t-cwt-qr	Notes
5-6	2 ×	2-0	7-0	1-11	3-1-2 ⎫	enclosed section
5-7	2 ×	2-0	7-0	1-11	⎬	11ft 0in long
5-8		2-8	7-0	1-11		all enclosed
5-8		3-6*	7-0	1-11	2-11-2	
5-8		3-6*	7-0	1-11	2-13-0	
5-8		4-9	7-0	1-11†	3-2-0	†as 2ft 6in gauge
–		9-8	5-6	1-11	1-15-2	
–		3-0	5-6	1-11		
–		–	4-0	1-11	1-16-0	5ft 4in over stanchions
		–	4-0	1-11	2-2-0	
–		1-8	5-6	1-11	1-16-0	six-plank wagons
–		7-9	4-0	1-11		were 1in higher

such as doorhandles or steps. Clearance of brakevans over steps is 6ft 6in. Brakevan
newly fitted sliding doors.

WELSHPOOL & LLANFAIR LIGHT RAILWAY PRESERVATION CO. LTD.

DIAMOND JUBILEE PASSENGER SERVICE RE-OPENING
6th April 1963

Llanfair Caereinion 6d to **Castle Caereinion**
AND BACK

Valid on day of issue only

Issue subject to the Coy's regulations, conditions and notices.

NOT TRANSFERABLE № 709

WELSHPOOL & LLANFAIR LIGHT RAILWAY PRESERVATION CO. LTD.

FIRST CLASS PASS
for use between
LLANFAIR CAEREINION & WELSHPOOL (RAVEN SQUARE)

VALID UNTIL _____

_____ CHAIRMAN

_____ SECRETARY

Issue subject to the Coy's regulations, conditions and notices.

NOT TRANSFERABLE N° 406

Signature of Holder _____

WELSHPOOL & LLANFAIR LIGHT RAILWAY PRESERVATION CO., LTD.

SYLFAEN TO LLANFAIR CAEREINION

Issued subject to the Company's regulations and notices. NOT TRANSFERABLE.

0404

W191—Williamson, Ticket Pri... ...ahton

WELSHPOOL & LLANFAIR LIGHT RAILWAY PRESERVATION CO., LTD.

(CHILD) LLANFAIR CAEREINION TO HENIARTH

Issued subject to the Company's regulations and notices. NOT TRANSFERABLE.

0428

W191 Williamson, Ticket Pri ...ahton

Gt Western Ry
CHEAP TICKET
For day of issue & BY
CERTAIN TRAINS ONLY
Llanf'r Caereinion
TO S.00
WELSHPOOL
SEVEN STARS
THIRD CLASS
ON BACK W.L.

6200

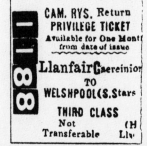

CAM. RYS. Return
PRIVILEGE TICKET
Available for One Mont[h]
from date of issue
Llanfair Caereinio[n]
TO
WELSHPOOL (S. Stars
THIRD CLASS
Not
Transferable (H
Llw

8118

Specimen tickets

Bibliography and sources

PRINTED BOOKS AND ARTICLES

Beyer Peacock Quarterly review 4 No 4 (1930)
Building News April and May 1901
Daily Express 9 February 1931
Eddowes Shrewsbury Journal 1886
J. Elwyn Davies *A Guide to Welshpool* (Welshpool, 1969), Official Guide.
J. D. K. Lloyd (editor) *Official County Handbook of Montgomeryshire*
Journal of the Transport Ticket Society No 19 (July 1965)
E. O. Mawson & E. R. Calthrop *Pioneer Irrigation and Light Railways* (1904)
The Montgomeryshire Collections, Transactions of the Powys-land Club esp. 44, 46, 48, 51
Montgomeryshire County Times 1931, 1952
The Montgomeryshire Express (formerly *Newtown and Welshpool Express*) Various dates 1875–1956.
Oswestry and Border Counties Advertizer (formerly *The Oswestry Advertizer and Montgomeryshire Mercury* and *The Oswestry Advertizer and Montgomeryshire Herald*) Various dates 1862–1931.
Transactions of the Newcomen Society, 24 'Early railways of the Ellesmere and Montgomeryshire Canals, 1794–1914'.
Railway Magazine 103 (1957)
The Railway Times August 1845
A review of Population Changes in Mid-Wales 1901–51 (1959)
Slezak. *Schmalspurig durch Osterreich* (1962)
Trains Illustrated 9 (1956)
Welshpool & Llanfair Light Railway Preservation Co Ltd, Publications. *Newsletter* (1957–68), *The Earl* (1959–67), *The Llanfair Railway Journal* (1968 on)

MANUSCRIPTS AND DOCUMENTS

British Transport Historical Records. Cambrian Railways Act, 1913, 3 & 4 Geo 5; Minute books of the Welshpool and Llanfair Light Railway Co; Report on Branch Lines, GWR, 1926; Service Timetables (Cambrian Railways and GWR); Welshpool and Llanfair Light Railway Order 1899, Amendment Order 1901, Further Borrowing Powers Order 1905.

House of Lords Record Office. Minutes of Select Committee on Railway Bills, H. C. 1866, Shrewsbury & North Wales Railway (Meifod Extension Bill); an Act to incorporate a company to construct a railway from Welshpool to Llanfair, 50–51 Vict c 185 (1887).

National Library of Wales. Deposited records of Montgomeryshire County Council: An Act to authorise the construction of a railway in the County of Montgomery from Welshpool to Llanfair, 40–41 Vict c 225 (1877); Plans, sections and books of reference, various schemes 1845–97. Montgomeryshire Scrapbooks 1896–98

M. M. Polglaze's collection of MSS relating to W & L.

Public Record Office. Board of Trade Railways Department, Correspondence and Papers.

University of Birmingham. Surveys relating to W & L (1966 & 1971) Welshpool & Llanfair Light Railway Co. Shareholders reports Welshpool & Llanfair Light Railway Preservation Co Ltd, collected MSS and plans

Authors' archive material.

Index

Illustrations are indicated by italics.
Stations and halts are grouped together, as are locomotives.